In Search of Modern Indian Identity
Through Architecture with Jugal Kishore Chowdhury

Edited By

Piyush Das

Manjari Gupta

Uday Bhanu Pattanayak

 COPAL publishing

Published by

Copal Publishing Group

E-143, Lajpat Nagar, Sahibabad,

Distt. Ghaziabad, UP – 201005, India

www.copalpublishing.com

Edited by:

Piyush Das

Manjari Gupta

Udaya Bhanu Pattanaik

Supported by:

Jugal Kishore Chowdhury Charitable & Educational Trust

Photographs by:

Mahatta & Co holds the copyright of all the photographs used in this book unless and until specified.

First Published 2019

© Copal Publishing Group 2018

ISBN: 978-93-83419-661 (Print)

Typeset by Bhumi Graphics, New Delhi

Printed and bound by Bhavish Graphics, Chennai

Preface

Padmashri Jugal Kishore Chowdhury belonged to the first generation of architects in post-independent India. As such, he was one of the path finders who energised the initiation of aspiring Indian architects to the world of modern architecture. His outstanding contributions in architecture and town planning is a legacy from which generations of young architects can reap rich dividends.

The Jugal Kishore Chowdhury Charitable and Educational Trust has, since its inception, made a concentrated effort to create a renewed interest and focus in the architectural masterpieces created by him. A lot of research has been done to know and understand JKC, the architect, the man and his mind. Through old friends, colleagues, family and students, a substantial amount of information has been compiled, regarding his work and his life.

Professional impeccability apart, JKC emerges from these findings as a fascinating personality with diverse interests.

The time in which JKC lived and worked was a time of remarkable resurgence and experimentation as far as Indian architecture is concerned. The corpus of his work bears testimony to the vibrant atmosphere he worked in. In the initial stages of his career, he worked as the Chief Architect of the Government of Punjab. This was the time when he worked with his mentor, the legendary Le Corbusier, who influenced him profoundly. Both collaborated in the making of Chandigarh.

However, it is his later works that showcase his unique originality and speak volumes of his creativity as a maverick architect and artist. An in-depth analysis about his work has been attempted in this book.

The first JKC memorial Lecture and an exhibition of his work were successfully held in Guwahati in 2015. It was followed by one in Ansal University, NCR of Delhi, in 2017. The JKC Trust and Ansal University have also inaugurated the Jugal Kishore Chowdhury Gallery of Architecture and the Arts in February 2018, to exhibit pioneering works in these fields.

We feel privileged to catalogue a segment of his remarkable achievements through this book. We also look forward to further delving into the infinite potential that his body of work provides.

Acknowledgement

This book would not have been possible without the support/ help/guidance of Jugal Kishore Chowdhury charitable and educational trust. We would like to thank Ranjit Chowdhary, and all the other trustees for providing support whenever needed. We would like to acknowledge the support of Prof. Nalini Thakur and Vijay Garg without whose help the project and research would not have been possible. It is with them that the whole idea of the exhibition on JKC and this book crystallized and took shape.

We sincerely thank SPA Delhi and Prof Chetan Vaidya, who helped us at the initial research on the work of JKC. The personal and professional experiences shared by S.N. Chowdhury (Brother of JKC), Ranjit Chowdhury (Nephew of JKC), S.K. Garella (Structural Engineer), A. Maitra , A.M. Ganju, Bibhuti Bhushan Chowdhury (Structural engineer), Abhijit Ray, Shovan K Shah, Prabir Halder, Rajeev Maini, Rajat Ray, Jitender Vats are indeed precious for the book. The Journal of the Indian Institute of Architects, May-June 1995 helped us with very articulate descriptions of some of JKC's work. For that along with others we thank Anil Nagrath (Editor, Journal of IIA, 1995) and Harshad Bhatia (Associate Editor, Journal of IIA, 1995). The interview of Jugal Kishore Chowdhury taken by Atul Gupta and Abhijit Ray in 1995 has helped us understanding JKC's own approach towards space making.

Abhijit Ray has also given us invaluable time and help in understanding JKC's persona and his work as an Architect. As the projects designed by JKC have under gone many changes and not much record in terms of drawings is available , the inputs from the persons who worked and interacted with him has helped us put together JKC's work and catalogue it.

Mahatta and Co. has generously helped us with sharing the very valuable photographs of buildings, drawings and sketches taken by Madan Mahatta. The first Jugal Kishore Chowdhury Memorial Lecture was held in Jan 2015 in Guwahati and the second one was held in Feb 2018 at Sushant school of Art & Architecture, Ansal University. We would like to thank The Vice Chancellor, Dr. Kamlesh Mishra and The Dean, SSAA Dr. Vibhuti Sachdev and her team for always supporting us.

Foreword

For us as young professionals of the 1950's, J.K. Chowdhury Saheb was a father figure in the realm of Architecture and Urban Design. It was therefore an honour to be closely associated with him in the mid-1960s as Joint Secretary, Institute of Town Planners, India, during his tenure as President of a compact but effective professional Institute. His penchant for looking at built form within the fast changing footprints of settlements in India, uniquely shaped many design and planning thoughts. It stood me well in my career which saw me through challenging assignments as Planning Commissioner of the Delhi Development Authority, Chief Planner of the Town and Country Planning Organisation and Director of the School of Planning and Architecture, Delhi.

In his twilight years, my family and I spent several lighter evenings at his Jor Bagh abode to be enlightened by his reminiscences of providing India with several and varied emulative designs within a context. The young and not so young are indebted to this self made ethical professional from Assam. His vision of total sustainable design encompassing Architecture, Urban Design and Spatial Development Planning is today central to the recently enacted National Schools of Planning & Architecture Act and which is to guide the gen-next towards an appropriate built form for a nation on the move.

It is heartening to know that this gen have recognised Jk Chowdhury Saheb role in this process.

Edgar F. Ribeiro

(EDGAR . F. RIBEIRO)
25/12/2014

Content

1

Introducing
Jugal Kishore Chowdhury
The Heart of the Matter

Jugal Kishore Chowdhury was born in 1918, in Goalpara district, Assam (India). His father Late Sobha Ram Chowdhury was from Batorhat in Kamrup district, while his mother Late Soudamini Chowdhury was from Goalpara town.

He completed his school education from Goalpara town, passing the matriculation examination in the first division and later completed his ISc examination from Cotton College, Guwahati.

According to S N Chowdhury (younger brother of Jugal Kishore Chowdhury), J K C was very ambitious as a child.

"He used to go to the bank of river Brahmaputra for jogging every day. He was very particular about physical fitness. As I was almost ten years younger to him, I have always seen him as a guardian. He was a man of style. He really made a man out of me. He got me married; he gave me a better life and stood by me forever. Both personally and professionally I have great respect for him."

After obtaining a degree in Civil Engineering from Lucknow, his professional education in Architecture started in Bombay where he completed his graduation from Sir J.J. School of Art. When asked regarding his choice of profession, J. K. Chowdhury said, "The colonial buildings in Shillong impressed me. They were designed by British architects using local materials to suit local climatic conditions. An article published by Principal of Engineering College, Spinet (now in Bangladesh), inspired me to pursue the study in architecture at Sir J.J. School of Architecture. I discontinued my studies in the third year and joined the freedom movement. I missed one year but thereafter I decided to proceed to England for completing my studies in Architecture and Town Planning at the Bartlett School of Architecture and Town Planning, University College, London. I was encouraged by late Lord Holford, my professor in Town Planning to pursue further studies of Regional Planning at the University of Tennessee and also to work in Tennessee Valley Authority (TVA) in the USA."

After completing his education in the USA, he had the privilege of working with the world famous architect Antonin Raymond in New York. He also served as an Associate Architect of Tennessee Valley Authority in the USA.

While working in the USA, he married late Eulie Suxena (Chowdhury), his architect colleague, who was the daughter of then Indian High Commissioner in the USA. The International Archive of Women in Architecture mentions her as the first woman to qualify as an architect in Asia. Eulie Chowdhury (nee Suxena) was the Chief Architect of Chandigarh (1971–76), and of Punjab (1976–81) and Haryana (1970–71).[1]

J. K. Chowdhury returned to India in 1949 and became the Chief Architect of the Kandla Port Township. He became the Chief Architect of Punjab Government (1950–1957), and made valuable contribution in the development of Chandigarh along with Le Corbusier and Pierre Jeanneret. In 1957, J.K. Chowdhury resigned from the government service and started practicing in Delhi where he established a firm in the name of "Chowdhury & Guljar Singh" at 1, Scindia House, Connaught place, New Delhi, a premise handed over to him by Sir Walter George before he left for England permanently.

---

[1] House that was Eulie's home *Posted on Sep 1st, 2009 in Middles* (http://www.roopinder.com/house-that-was-eulies-home/)

Figure 1 Marriage ceremony of Jugal Kishore Chowdhury and Eulie Suxena [*Source*: Collection of JKC Trust]

Figure 2 Eulie Suxena and Jugal Kishore Chowdhury [*Source*: Collection of JKC Trust]

Figure 3 J. K. Chowdhury having a discussion in design with Eulie Chowdhury [*Source*: Collection of JKC Trust]

Not many families are blessed with members who are aspirationally different, who are born with ideals and dreams which transcend the stereotype. And almost eight decades ago, only a select few dared to wander beyond attested bounds to choose a road less frequented. Jugal Kishore Chowdhury, better known as JKC to his world, was one such person. He was my father's much loved elder brother.

My first childhood impressions of JKC were tinted by the force of his personality. For all of us, he was a larger than life figure. He was different from the other elders that I had known. His occasional visits to Assam created a flurry of excitement in our big extended family. To my young mind, he seemed like an exotic knight in shining armour, returning home for a short while before setting off once again on adventures new!

3

By the time I could understand the ways of the world, his career as an architect had already been established. My father, who idolized him, proudly regaled us with stories about his determined crusade to chart out an unusual destiny for himself... away from home and everything familiar! His work, his achievements, his social life, his friends etc. – all these provided interesting snippets that captivated our imagination. In our equable existence, these anecdotes helped to sculpt him into an intrepid and charismatic personality, thereby stimulating our malleable minds.

Whenever JKC came to Assam, he stayed with us and the family reunions became the high points of our childhood. I would be deeply disappointed if his visits did not coincide with my holidays as I was in boarding school in Shillong. He was fiercely critical of most of us and his acerbic comments spared none! His standards were very high and most often, we failed to satisfy his exacting demands. It was much later in life that we understood the censure was to urge us youngsters to scale frontiers beyond the staid and the ordinary.

Yet underneath the forbidding demeanour, there was a soft core in him regarding my father's children. He liked spirited people. Those who could voice an opinion. And my feisty sisters could always draw a smile from him. To my siblings and me, therefore, he always remained our "Jetha" (elder uncle) and a constant source of wonder and admiration for the kind of life he led. And also because of the vast trajectory of his experiences!

My years in college were spent in Delhi and this led to a closer interaction with JKC. He kept an immaculate home even though he lived alone by then as he and his wife had parted company. However, he was always appreciative of the contribution she had made both to his career and to his personal life.

Jetha's circle of friends was like the Who's Who of Delhi in those days. He loved learning and assiduously cultivated friends from all walks of life. Besides his chosen profession, he was deeply interested in art, sociology, history, music and, most importantly, education. I had to endure highly intellectual discussions at the dining table whenever I visited him and had to respond with critical intelligence! Reading the newspaper thoroughly was a must. Otherwise, I would be grilled about the politics of the time just because he wanted to keep tabs on my awareness! These situations definitely did not appeal to the callow youth I was then. But on hindsight, I realised that he did it with the purpose of giving me a more rounded education than any college could offer. The quality time that I was literally forced to spend with him has paid me rich dividends in my life till now.

JKC was a fascinating blend of inborn and acquired talents. He loved beauty in all forms. I remember once how he was bowled over by Rekha's beauty after watching the film "Umrao Jaan" with my wife. His sartorial elegance and appreciation for fine living became a lifelong compulsion and he fitted in effortlessly in the cultural and social world of the metropolis, so different from his roots.

Reminiscences about JKC could fill a book! There are so many stories about his quirky nature, his cynical humour. He was never a conformist and lived life on his terms. Yet, he was there for the family when they needed him. A very private man, he invited my wife, daughter and me to spend holidays with him several times. Meticulous in everything as he was on the drawing board, he would write down the recipe of each dish my wife cooked for him for future reference. He even took note of simple facts such as that cut flowers lasted longer if the water in the vase was changed frequently!

He was devoted to his association with Delhi Public School,

specially DPS, R. K. Puram. Perhaps because of his own chequered education, he valued academic excellence highly and gravitated to people who promoted it. He consciously encouraged research and was deeply interested in sponsoring young scholars to delve into the authentic origins of his community. The goal for him was to affirm the truth of history.

JKC was a man ahead of his times professionally. His contributions to Indian Architecture and Town Planning have been acknowledged during his lifetime and much lauded recently. This recognition from his peers would have warmed his heart certainly. His architectural achievements are a legacy he left behind for the wider public world. He perhaps believed Julia Morgan when she said, "My buildings will ....speak for me long after I'm gone." A story I heard from my aunt is that when Jetha was forty and still single, his mother fretted that he would never have children. He told her that the buildings he created were his children!

As his nephew and someone who was as close to him as was possible, I can only speak of him from a familial perspective.

He enriched our lives in many subtle ways. Certain gestures made by him still resonate in my mind. A year or two before he passed away , he gifted my wife and daughter with a book on modern art which had been in his possession for more than forty years, inscribing in it the following words: "The human mind is never static...It flows back and forth in time. Hence all art forms are inseparably related, including architecture." This sums up the measure of the man and his mind.

For us, his legacy is not what he left behind for people, but the imprint he left behind in us, whose lives he touched. He set high benchmarks for the rest of the family regarding commitment, dedication and the striving for excellence.
Such is the 'man' etched in our minds and the many stories about him which we can share with others to perpetuate the memory of an extraordinary life.

The heart of the matter by Ranjit Kumar Chowdhury (retd professor of English, Cotton College, Guwahati and nephew of Jugal Kishore Chowdhury)

2

Projects, Institutional Involvement, Awards and Memberships

Significant Projects

Master Plan, Chandigarh (with Le Corbusier)
Regional Engineering College Campus, Chandigarh
Master Plan, Punjab University
State Bank of India building, Chandigarh
Punjab National Bank, Chandigarh
University Personnel Housing, Chandigarh
Main College Building, Ludhiana Agricultural University
IIT Delhi
Guwahati Medical College, Assam
Dibrugarh University, Assam
Silchar Medical College and Hospital, Assam
Hindustan Fertilizer, Rohtak Road
Institute of Catering Technology & Hotel Management, Delhi
Chandigarh, BRD project
Rajendra Agricultural University, Bihar
Convention Centre and Annexe, Ashoka Hotel, New Delhi
Office Building at Chanakyapuri, New Delhi
Haryana Agricultural University, Hisar
Medical College and Hospital, Jammu
LNJP and Maulana Azad Medical College, Delhi
LNJP Orthopaedic block, GB Pant Hospital, Delhi

Figure 4 J K Chowdhury

New Secretariat Building, Srinagar
New University of Jammu
Regional Engineering College campus, Ludhiana
Ingot factory, Jalandhar
Nangal Township buildings
Nangal Fertilizers and Chemical Factories
The Bharat Coking Coal Limited (BCCL) Township, Dhanbad

Institutional Involvement

Member, Indian Delegation of Hotel Industries to Japan and the U.S.A. (1963)

Vice President, Indian Institute of Town Planners (1963–64)

Participated in the World Congress on Housing and Town Planning, Israel, representing the Indian Institute of Town planners (1964)

President, Indian Institute of Town Planners (1964–65 and 1965–66)

Leader, Delegation of Architects and Town Planners to the Netherlands

Studied Housing and Town Planning in Sweden, Denmark, Germany, France and England (1966)

Participated in the 34th World Congress, International Federation for Housing and Planning, Hamburg (1978)

Participated in the 35th World Congress, Gothenburg (1983)

Participated in the 37th World Congress in Berlin (West) (1984)

International Congress in Budapest in Hungary; Studied problems of metropolitan regions in Vienna, Frankfurt, Berlin, Paris (1985)

24th Congress of the International Society of City & Regional Planners, Taormina, Sicily (1988)

Awards

Winner of the All India Township Competition for Bharat Coking Coal Ltd. Township, Dhanbad (1974)

Padma Shri Award from the President of India (1977)

Recipient of the "Distinguished Services Award" by the Senate, Indian Institute of Technology, Delhi (1986)

Baburao Mhatre Award (1995)

Membership of Professional Bodies

Fellow of the Indian Institute of Architects (FIIA)
Fellow of the Royal Institute of British Architects (FRIBA)
Fellow of the Royal Town Planning Institute (FRTPI), London
Fellow of the Institute of Town Planners, India

3

Post-Independence Indian Identity Through Architecture

India saw significant changes in its architectural identity after independence. The first three decades after independence provided the potential to propel the nation towards building a new modernity in Indian architecture. This was impelled by the first generation of post-independence architects.

During this time there were three different categories of Indian architects and architecture. First were the architects whose work evolved from the early 20th century outlook towards a modernist approach. Then there was a group of architects who had grown out of the Art Deco. Thereafter there were the architects who had foreign degrees and had international exposure.

In the years following independence, all Indian architects were involved in building a new India in tune with the heady spirit of the times. Architects of that era were inspired by this spirit to visualize Indian Architecture in a modern way.

Many architects of this generation came back to India after studying abroad. Some of them had worked under the masters of the modern movement. They transferred their experiences to Indian projects in terms of values and symbols of modernity.

The architecture which thus emerged was modern in conception, yet infusing in the creations a strong Indian Identity.

In this rebuilding of the new identity many foreign architects were also invited. One of them was Le Corbusier for the new state capital – Chandigarh. He consciously attempted to break the past 'historicism' of imperial architecture. As he had once written to his wife "it will be a city of trees, of flowers and water, of houses as simple as those at the time of Homer, and of a few splendid edifices of the highest level of modernism, where the rule of mathematics will reign".

Out of the many architects who worked with Corbusier in the making of Chandigarh, Jugal Kishore Chowdhury was one of the foremost. He was the Chief Architect of Punjab Government from 1950 to 1957, and made valuable contributions in the development of Chandigarh along with Le Corbusier and Pierre Jeanneret.

When India achieved freedom, a resurgence was felt in all aspects of public life. The first generation of architects set the foundation for a fresh, new and modern identity to the architecture of the country. Jugal Kishore Chowdhury was assuredly one of those pioneering architects who imprinted a significant and powerful impress upon this quest for modernity. He addressed the spirit of the times instead of following historical precedents to create a new Indian Architectural Identity. Through his projects, we can see a compelling narrative which is uniquely Indian and deeply rooted in the local traditions. He made us realize that when form, function and construction technology are integrally conceived and executed, how beautiful architectural creations can become.

[2] A Concise History of Modern Architecture in India by Jon. T. Lang, p. 31

[3] The Age of Indian Architecture After Independence by Vishal Kumar, blog. 27th July 2015

[4] Letter to his wife Yvonne, 27 February 1951, FLC-R1-12-87.

4

Search for Singularity: Work in 1950s and Early 1960s

Before joining the Punjab Government in 1950, J. K. Chowdhury had already worked for the Kandla Port Township project as the Chief Architect. The Punjab University master plan was designed by him, which was later revised by Pierre Jeanneret and B P Mathur later. He was also the architect of the early campus buildings of the university. Before he left the government service in 1957, he had already designed the College of Chemical Engineering and Technology, a temporary office building and five hundred houses for university personnel of the Chandigarh University. In 1957, J. K. Chowdhury resigned from government service and started practice at Delhi where he established a firm (bought over the practice of Architect Walter George[5]) in the name of "Chowdhury & Gulzar Singh" at 1, Scindia House, Connaught place, New Delhi. Some of the projects designed in the early 1960s were the office building at Chanakyapuri and Master plan for Dibrugarh University.

Chemical Engineering College, Chandigarh

Choice of materials, visual connections and climatically responsive design such as jaali corridors were commendable aspects in the design of the Chemical Engineering College at Chandigarh by J. K. Chowdhury

Figure 5 Well-lit and ventilated curvilinear corridor with brick *jaali* of the Chemical Engineering Department [*Photograph*: Piyush Das]

[5] Walter Sykes George (1881–1962) was an English Architect. He was in the team of architects who designed New Delhi.

Figure 6 A unique stone masonry of one of the walls with a prominent stone spout of the Chemical Engineering Department of Punjab University showcasing the use of indigenous material. [*Photograph*: Piyush Das]

Figure 7 Brick *Jali* work seen from the outside [*Photograph*: Piyush Das]

Figure 8 Build form defining vision and adding character to build space
[*Photograph*: Piyush Das]

Office Building at Chanakyapuri in 1960s

Jugal Kishore Chowdhury was appointed upon the initiatives of Prime Minister Lal Bahadur Shastri to design the office building at Chanakyapuri. Visually, in terms of the design, the building symbolised the free spirit of a free nation, the tower-like structure adding a sense of grandeur. The façade on all four sides was covered with vertical louvers giving sun shading. The proportion in which the building was vertically divided is striking even today.

Figure 9 Office building at Chanakyapuri

Dibrugarh University 1965

The planning of the campus of Dibrugarh University was executed keeping the topography and the natural landscape in mind. The lakes within the site and the Botanical garden at the west side add character to the site. The existing heritage structure with the tank was kept as it is with landscaping around it (2 in the development plan). The academic block at the north west side had the main departments with interconnecting courtyards.

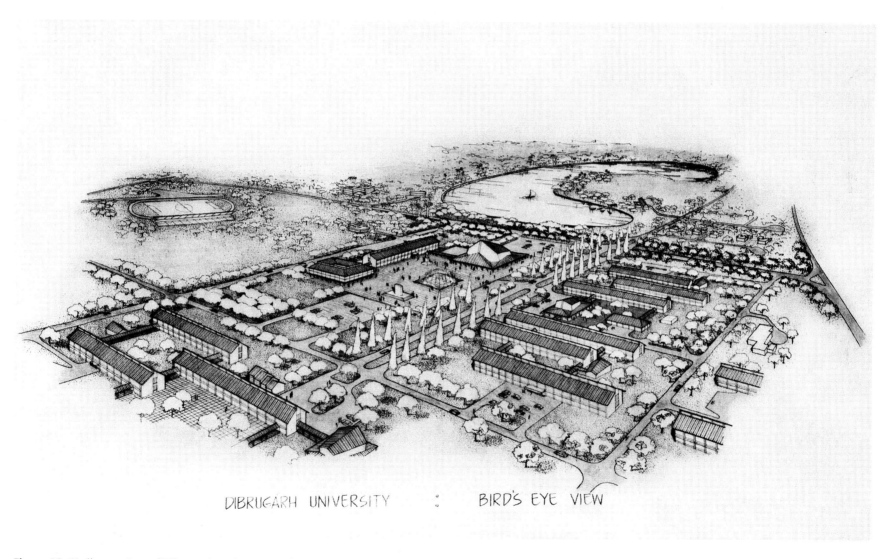

DIBRUGARH UNIVERSITY : BIRD'S EYE VIEW

Figure 10 Bird's eye view of Dibrugarh University with the southern side lake in the vicinity

1	EXISTING GUEST HOUSE
2	EXISTING MONUMENT WITH TANK
3	SCIENCE THEATRES
4	ARTS THEATRES
5	TECHNOLOGY THEATRES
6	STADIUM
7	BOYS HOSTELS
8	GIRLS HOSTELS
9	CLINIC
10	COOLING TANK
11	PROFESSORS QUARTERS
12	STAFF QUARTERS
13	SHOPPING CENTRE & POST OFFICE ETC
14	STUDENT ACTIVITY CENTRE WITH SWIMMING POOL
15	STAFF CLUB
16	SCHOOL
17	UNDERPASS
18	MAIN ENTRY GATE
19	LAKE
20	BOTANICAL GARDEN

DEVELOPMENT PLAN   DIBRUGARH UNIVERSITY

MS CHOWDHURY & GULZAR SINGH   ARCHITECTS   TOWN PLANNERS   STRUCTURAL ENGINEERS   &   CONSULTANTS

Figure 11 Development Plan for Dibrugarh University

5

Established Individuality: Work in Late 1960s, IIT Delhi

By the mid-1960s, Jugal Kishore Chowdhury had already established an individuality in his architectural expressions. He strongly believed in "form follow function". As he said once, "To me every building is a challenge to produce a work of art and originality".

Structural Engineer, S K Garella who worked with JKC from 1965 to 1969 recalls his approach towards designing to be very sensitive.

"He was a much respected man in the field and very well connected. I have been groomed there and that experience stood by me all through my life. He lived in style and he was a man of class. One of the most sensitive and functional architect I have ever known in my life. J K Chowdhury planned everything, whether it is small building or a large campus; he used to plan all the stages very efficiently. As a structural engineer though my involvement was more with his partner Guljar Singh but he was an inspiration for me and will be forever."

Ashoka Hotel Convention Centre, New Delhi 1966

Government proposal to host UNCTAD Conference in 1966 demanded additional expanse of the existing Ashoka Hotel, New Delhi, whose architecture was traditional in nature. Jugal Kishore Chowdhury responsibly took the job and designed the Convention Center.

Prof Maitra ,Ex-Director, SPA Delhi who worked with J. K. Chowdhury during the mid-1960s and was involved in the design of the Convention center compliments him to be an architect par excellence. His reminiscences are worth recalling,

"Though I have worked with him for one and half year but for the rest of my life, till his sad demise, he was like a fatherly figure for me both personally and professionally. He was an architect with strong function-oriented design, and was a fantastic teacher. J K Chowdhury used to sketch a lot and used to spend lots of time in detailing out a plan in sketches. The product which evolved was worth seeing. It was a great experience working with him. He was a modern architect and surprisingly though he worked in Chandigarh with Corbusier, but he was never influenced. He had his own creativity and originality."

Figure 12 Expansion of Ashoka Hotel

Figure 13 The proposed revolving tower (not executed), Ashoka Hotel

Figure 14 View of the Convention Center, Ashoka Hotel

Figure 15 Perspective sketch of the Convention Center, Ashoka Hotel

Figure 16 Lobby in the Ashoka Hotel Convention Center

Figure 17 Lobby in the Ashoka Hotel Convention Center

Guwahati Medical College & Hospital

A. M. Ganju worked with J. K. Chowdhury for a very brief period in mid 1960s and was involved with projects such as Hisar Agricultural University, Expansion of Ashoka Hotel and Guwahati Medical College out of many. As he explains *"The architect who taught modern architecture to India was none other than Jugal Kishore Chowdhury. His buildings speak the language of modern architecture. He was an original thinker and an artist. He was innately proud of his* work and designs. He was dedicated and extremely talented. He believed in sketching and his drawings were very explanatory. He used to think in four dimensions, considering space with time. Though he worked with Corbusier and had a thoroughly Western experience, what he created on his own was original and showcases the exemplary concepts of contemporary architecture. Buildings designed by him are still considered contemporary. He was an architect with great sense of aesthetics."

Figure 18 A development perspective of the Guwahati Medical College

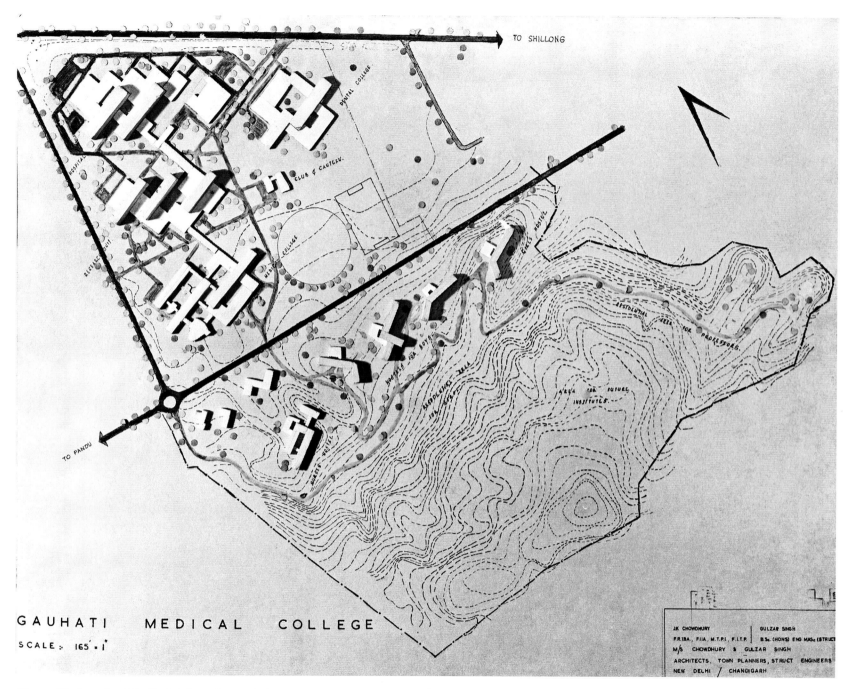

GAUHATI MEDICAL COLLEGE

SCALE :- 165' = 1"

TO SHILLONG

TO PANDU

JK CHOWDHURY | GULZAR SINGH
F.R.IBA., FIIA, M.T.P.I, F.I.T.P. | B.Sc (HONS) ENO MAS₂ (STRUCT
M/S CHOWDHURY & GULZAR SINGH
ARCHITECTS, TOWN PLANNERS, STRUCT ENGINEERS
NEW DELHI / CHANDIGARH

Figure 19 Guwahati Medical College & Hospital

21

The Guwahati Medical College was planned respecting the natural terrain. The southern part of the land was left vacant for future institutional expansion. All the major blocks like the Dental College, Research Unit, Medical College and the Hospital was planned accordingly and they were connected by series of courtyards. The medical block itself was planned with 6 interconnecting courtyards.

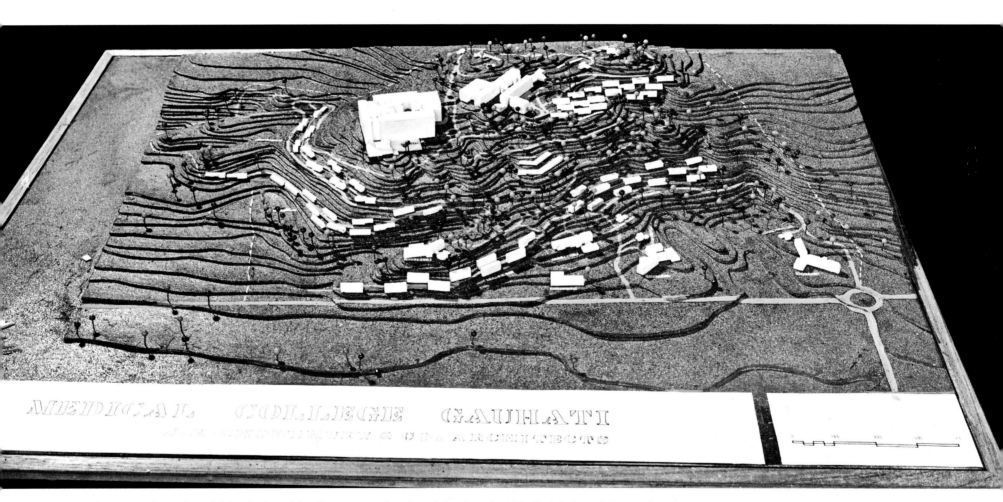

Figure 20 Physical model (preliminary) for the campus planning of the Guwahati Medical College & Hospital

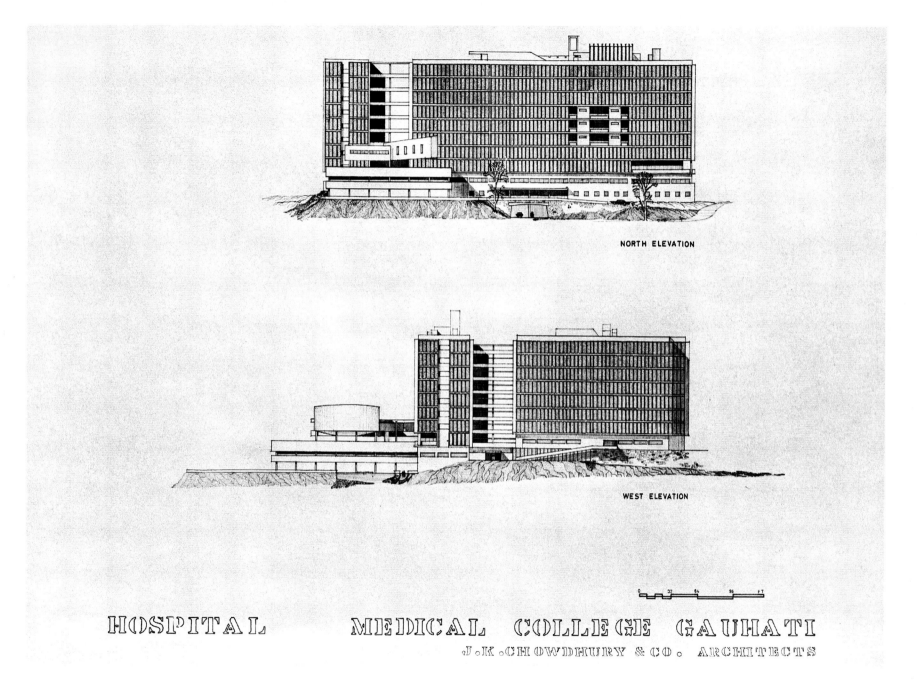

NORTH ELEVATION

WEST ELEVATION

HOSPITAL   MEDICAL COLLEGE GAUHATI

J.K.CHOWDHURY & CO. ARCHITECTS

Figure 21 North and West side elevation of the Main Hospital Building of Guwahati Medical College.

23

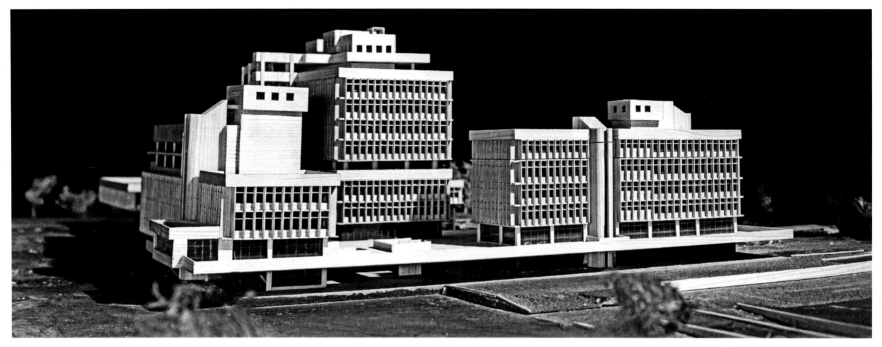

Figure 22 Preliminary stage physical models of Guwahati Medical College.

IIT Delhi 1968

(Description from Journal of The Indian Institute of Architects, May-June 1995, Volume 60, ISSUE 04)

The campus of the Indian Institute of Technology Delhi was designed with an essential urge to promote the scientific, technological and sociological progress of the country. Thus the country's premier Institute representing the highest quality to attain academic excellence needed to be sheltered in an environment to withstand the test of time. So thirty years after it has been completed, the campus can now be evaluated again.

The evaluation need not be based on the building itself in isolation, but in the understanding of the programme. The design of IIT Delhi emerged out of an analytical programming in which a Regional Engineering College was given the status of a premier National Institute. The assessment of future growth was visualized in a clear and imaginative manner by the architect planner with the help and collaboration of a team of British professors, specialized in the fields of science and technology. The design provides for a high degree of flexibility ensuring growth for the future.

A 320 acre site was acquired for the campus located at the foothills of Aravalli. The site has uneven slopes with low lying area. These areas often get flooded during severe rains forming 'nullahs' thus dividing the site into three distinct portions. The zoning of site was thus derived from the essential functional requirements of the campus which needed to house three distinct activities, viz.

the academic programme of the institute, the student housing and the residential quarters for the faculty and other staff. While the main academic area has been given a central location on a more or less flattened site between the natural drains, the residential area was located towards the eastern part, in close proximity to the city's arteries. The students were housed in the quarter western part with their social and recreational activities.

Designed to function as a major thrust area in the large scale urban setting of the campus, the theme of the academic zone essentially has been grouping of teaching and laboratory buildings in a manner that can impart the maximum functional efficiency, flexibility and economy.

The courses common to all the departments have been housed in one building resulting in a multi-storey block, a long rectangular building resting on one side on the two-storey administrative block with a Computer Centre and a Convention Hall and on the other three-storey main laboratories. Here is the architect's subjective design decision that played an important part producing a dynamic effect of form and function. The visual impact that is created in one's mind is the multi-storeyed building standing boldly facing the east and west sun demanding cladding of east and west facades with thin concrete-free standing louvers to protect the building from strong penetrating sun and the three-storey blocks at right angles with much needed north–south orientation

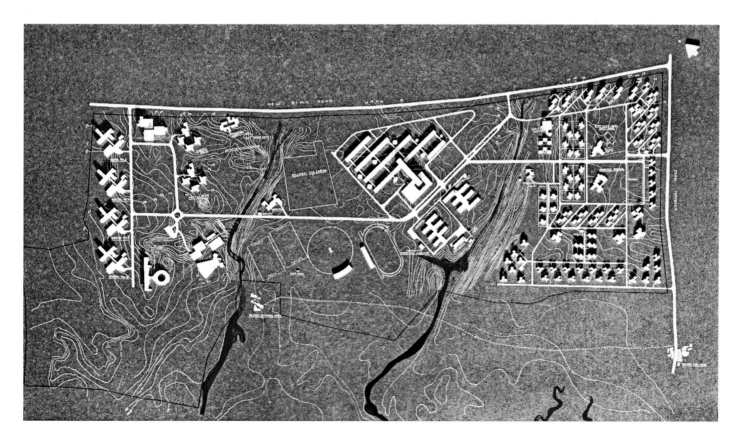

Figure 23 Physical model of the campus planning of IIT Delhi

to the main engineering laboratories which run parallel, linked by a system of corridors and covered walkways during sun and rains. The end of the laboratory blocks are left blank to make them free to extend anytime for expansion. The courtyards formed between the connecting corridors have been dotted with lecture theatres of different sizes each separately designed to be shared by the departments according to the capacity of the theatre and sizes of classes thus optimizing the utilization of the common facilities by the departments. The optimization of these common facilities is obtained with the help of centralized timetable.

As one enters the IIT gate from the main road, one is immediately struck by the impressive design of the gate, a cantilevered RCC flat arch standing on a single RCC inviting vehicular traffic through entry and pedestrian on either side. A visitor coming along with dual carriage way leading to the academic zone automatically gets attracted towards the multi-storey block towering the campus and bring him right under the stilted entrance of the classrooms and laboratories common to all the departments located in this tower block. The visual impact of the

Figure 24 Entry Gate: IIT Delhi

tower block is such that one need not have to search out the administrative and academic blocks.

In continuation of the road giving entry under the tower block, the entrance to the computer centre is easily noticed. The computer centre of the IIT is one of the best in the country which provides opportunities to the students to study up to PhD level.

Standing over the computer centre is the impressive convocation hall with a seating capacity of over 1500 students. The hyperbolic paraboloid instead of parabolic shell roof over the convocation hall is perhaps one of the unique designs of its kind in the world. The shape of this shell roof is such that it provides natural acoustic treatment. The architectural impact created by the well-proportioned shell roof of the convocation hall further highlights the artistic quality of the multi-storeyed block with its symphonic composition of the roof terrace approached by a lift and a ramp where students cafeteria, faculty lounge and restaurant are located providing a panoramic view of the entire campus as well as beyond, bringing the historic Qutab Minar closer. Added to this beautifully designed roof silhouette is the critically operated bell tower with its brass-gong donated by the British Government, providing an unique architectural composition rarely to be seen anywhere. The dual carriage way leading to the main entrance under the tower block, a little further away, provides access to the Central Library which is approached by an open staircase providing entry to the three-storeyed block at the 1st floor level. The library and the computer centre are linked by a beautifully designed corridor for easy communication to the students. The library designed for 30,000 books is one of the best libraries in the country, centrally air-conditioned and computerized. Located at a quiet place next to the computer centre, it is used throughout the day and late hours of the night. It is one of the most well-planned libraries, compact, efficient and economical architecturally, it has many characteristic features. The internal circulation system is very effective. Maximum use of daylight has been utilized.

Student Activity Centre

The heart of the students is felt in the design of the Students Activity Centre. Located away from the main institute building and the hostels, the building is a maze of students in the evenings. During the day the student committee member move around usually organizing the next social or the sports meet.

The building is low in the surroundings, and it is only when you actually move through the buildings that the building unfolds itself. A small floor bridge over the 'nullah' brings the visitors to the entrance door and as soon as you enter the ball the feel of its activities come forth as the foyer has a sculptured court indoor with a ramp moving up to the next floor. The floor levels change intricately with the foyer moving down into the music rooms on the right and the squash courts on the left, the pleasant transition of the indoor to the semi-covered walkway is a thoughtful element. The next building linking up through the passage is the gymnasium, which acts as a dance hall during the much celebrated 'Rendezvous' the annual festival of IIT. The regular usage of the gymnasium is however a strong point of success of the Students Activity Centre. Architecturally, it is a bold design with a strong character expressing the function.

Behind the Gymnasium is the open Air Theatre, which has been designed for a seating capacity of 2500 students, utilizing a low-lying area. This has added a very useful amenity to the students' cultural activities.

Hostel Buildings

Although a few day-Scholars are admitted, IIT is basically residential Institute. It has therefore, a number of hostel buildings for boys as well as girls. Each hostel is designed for 200 students with separate Dining Hall, Lounge, Games Room, Kitchen and a Warden's Quarter. Height of these buildings is restricted to 4 storeys without elevators. The hostels can be divided into 2 distinct groups, one group is of 13.5" load bearing walls of exposed brick structure and the other group is of RCC framed structure, strongly expressing their form with 2.6" wide projection all around the building to protect the 9" thick exposed brick walls on the exterior and 4.5" internal walls which provide flexibility for future change.

Choice of Materials

The cost of maintenance of buildings plays an important part at the very early stage of design. Local available materials are preferred not only to reduce the cost of buildings but also to preserve the regional architectural character. The local materials predominantly used are bricks and concrete. Sparingly, Dholpur stone slabs and rough stone aggregates are also used in some of the institutional buildings to add richness to them such as Lecture Theatres, the Administrative Block and the Central Library building. The local available brick being porous, the Dholpur stone slabs and rough stone aggregate finish over the 9" brick walls were used. These have provided a pleasant contrast with shutter finished concrete. JKC believes in expressing purity of form in his building and this is one of the strong points of his architecture.

In the residential buildings such as two-storey professor's quarters and four-storey staff quarters, mostly local bricks have been used without plaster, so as to reduce the annual cost of maintenance and provide freshness of natural colour of the bricks and avoid use of coloured cement paints. The architectural character of the residential buildings is bold and pleasing and stood the test of time.

The Director's bungalow, constructed on a small hillock, is one of the most successful designs. It has been well integrated with the site overlooking the residential colony. The strong architectural character of this building befits the position that the Director of the institute holds. The sculptural quality of the building constructs with its functional form provides a unique aesthetic appeal. Both in summer and winter, the IIT campus provides a restful environment disposition bold and beautiful covering large part of South Delhi and unique creation of a single architect's work over 35 years.[6]

[6] Journal of The Indian Institute of Architects, May-June 1995, Volume 60, ISSUE 04, Editor Anil Nagrath, Associate editor Harshad Bhatia

Figure 25 Hostel Building: IIT Delhi

Figure 26 Hostel Building: IIT Delhi

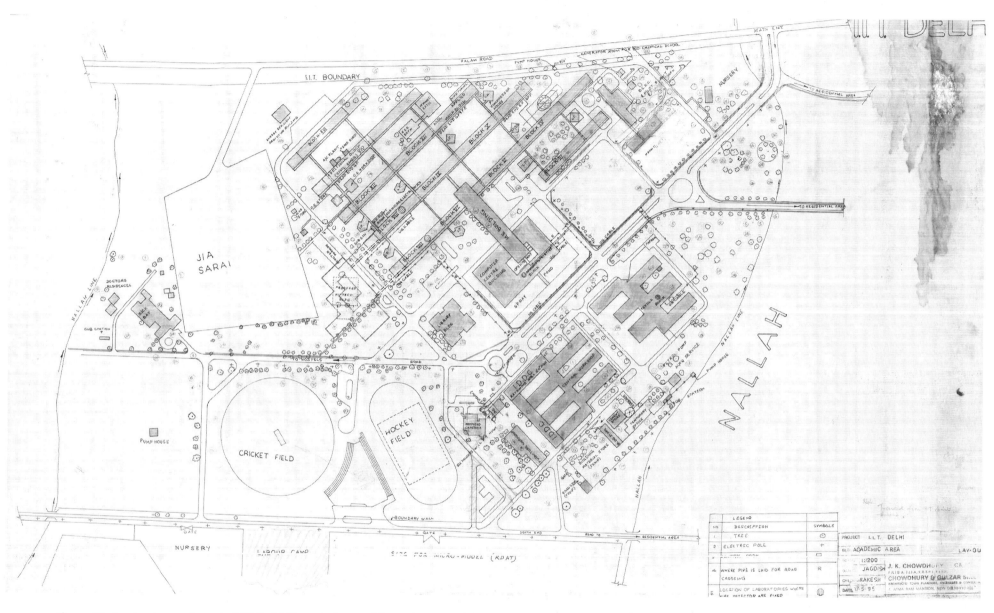

Figure 27 Academic area layout of IIT Delhi [*Source*: Scanned from the original drawings at Jor Bagh Residence of Jugal Kishore Chowdhury]

Figure 28 External staircase: IIT Delhi

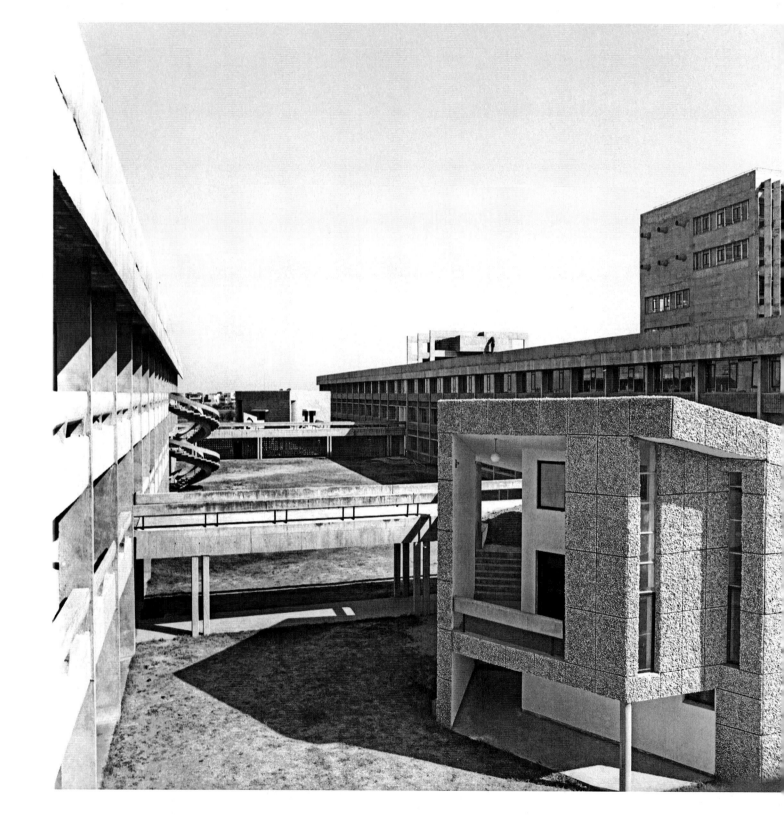

Figure 29 Bridges connecting the blocks: IIT Delhi

Figure 30 Mushroom Column: IIT Delhi

Figure 31 Swimming pool: IIT Delhi

Figure 32 J K Chowdhury believed in expressing purity in architecture: Use of rough stone aggregates finish

Figure 33 Open Air Theatre

Figure 34 Staff quarters: IIT Delhi

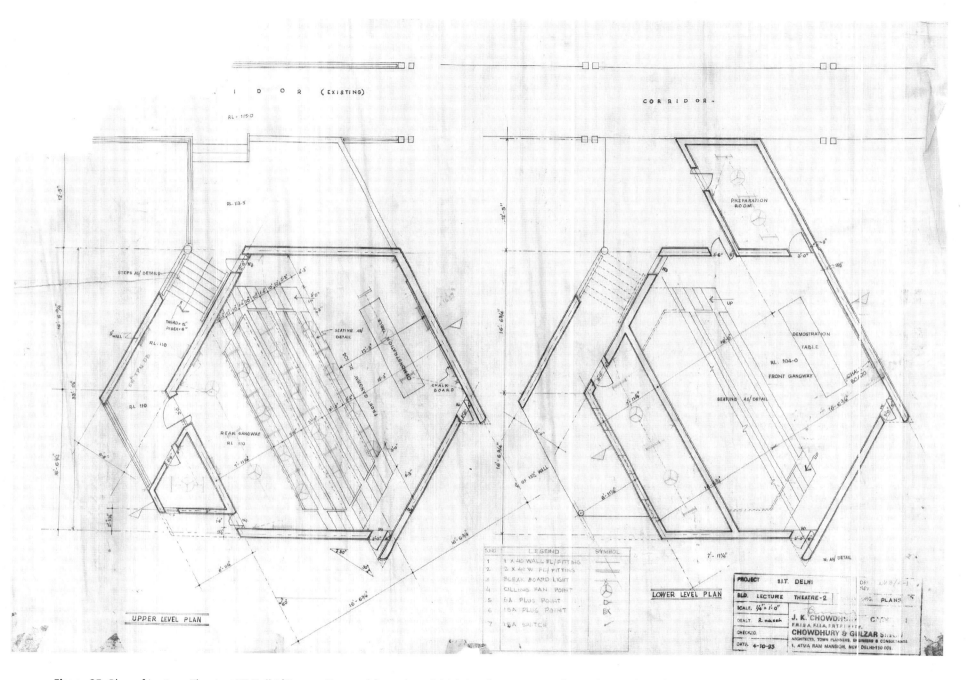

Figure 35 Plan of Lecture Theatre: IIT Delhi [*Source*: Scanned from the original drawings at Jor Bagh Residence of Jugal Kishore Chowdhury]

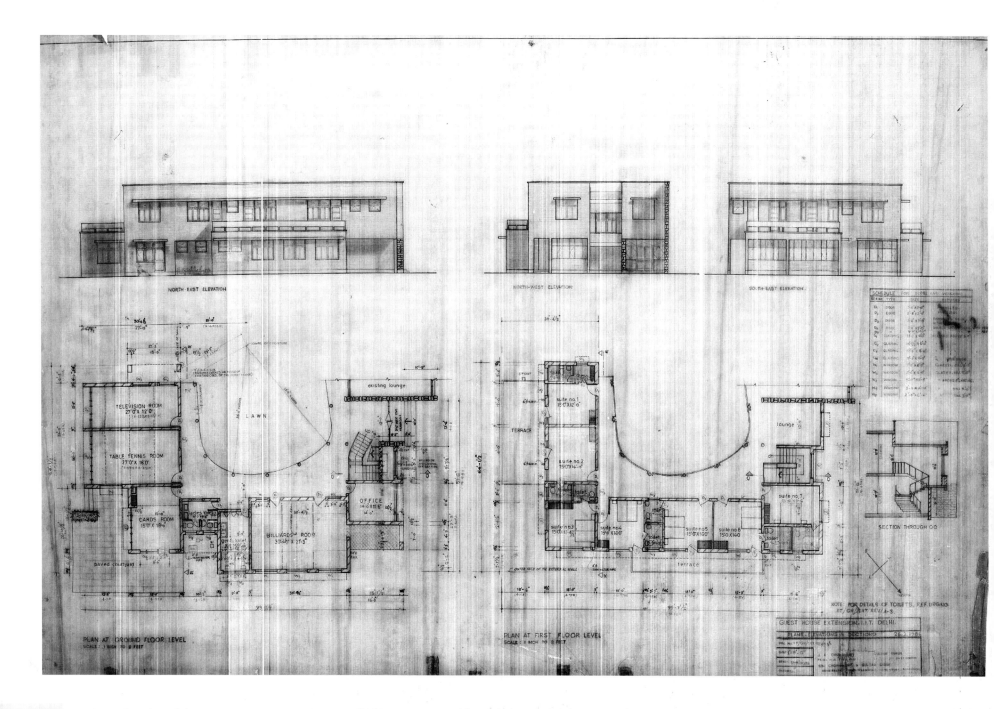

NORTH-EAST ELEVATION

NORTH-WEST ELEVATION

SOUTH-EAST ELEVATION

PLAN AT GROUND FLOOR LEVEL
SCALE : 1 INCH TO 8 FEET

PLAN AT FIRST FLOOR LEVEL
SCALE : 1 INCH TO 8 FEET

SECTION THROUGH OO

40 **Figure 36** Plan of the Guest House extension: IIT Delhi [*Source*: Scanned from the original drawings at Jor Bagh Residence of Jugal Kishore Chowdhury]

Figure 37 Eccentric external staircase design: IIT Delhi

41

Figure 38 Spiral staircase with wooden railing design in the interior spaces: IIT Delhi

Figure 39 Exposed concrete roof and columns in the interiors: IIT Delhi

Figure 40 Self-shading built designs: IIT Delhi

Figure 41 IIT Delhi

6

Master Architect and Visionary: 1970s and Other Works

"Jugal Kishore Chowdhury belonged to an era when architectural profession in India was at its infancy. It will be appreciated that in those days all drawings were hand drafted on the drawing board, tenders were types and cyclostyled, structural calculations were done with slide rules. Telephone lines were indifferent and STD calls a pain. These obviously imposed severe restrictions on human outputs. However with his natural flair of management, JKC fared extremely well with his team of fifteen architects, four structural engineers, two civil engineers, two electrical engineers, one plumbing engineer and other supporting staff (early 1970s). He has excelled in his assignments due to his in-depth working experience in building constructions and related topics.

He had an appreciable quality of working with the structural designer in evolving an optimum solution for the functional need of a building. In the Hisar Agricultural University project, the library has a flat slab system. Basic science buildings have a beam and slab system with defined pathway for piped gas and water. Space below window sill is used for horizontal run of service pipes. External columns are V shaped to give the building an identity. He always encouraged structural engineers to innovate a scheme that suited the functional need of the building.

The northeastern state is in the high seismic zone in India. JKC noted that the local construction consisted of wooden frames with verticals on either side of windows and horizontals at plinth, window sill, lintel and eaves level. The infilled panels were made up of "Icra" panels plastered on both faces. "Icra" is a local weed available in plenty. This way self-weight of the wall system reduced considerably. As seismic force on any structure is a function of its weight, low wall loads obviously attract lesser destabilizing forces, thus rendering the structure as safe. He proposed a similar system with 125 mm × 150 mm RCC verticals on either side of windows, and 125 mm × 150 mm horizontal bands at plinth, window sill, and lintel and eaves levels. Infilled panels are of brick work. JKC was always searching for the root cause of the problem to evolve a solution around it.

JKC made master plans honouring the planning brief of the clients. But he was fully aware of the ever increasing demands of our growing population and he kept a sublime provision for future expansion requirements. IIT Delhi and Guwahati Medical College & Hospital bear enough proof of this.

Structures handled by JKC were buildable even in remote locations. They have all withstood the test of time.

Jugal Kishore Chowdhury lived with his feet firmly on the ground and head at cloud nine to have a clear overview."

–Bibhuti Bhusan Chaudhuri worked with J K C as a structural engineer from 1969 to 1972

Haryana Agricultural University, Hisar, 1970s

(Description from Journal of The Indian Institute of Architects, May-June 1995, Volume 60, ISSUE 04)

In 1970, it was decided to convert the two existing colleges, Agricultural and Veterinary Sciences, at Hisar into a fully-fledged university. Accordingly, a comprehensive master plan was prepared for an eventual population of 25,000 – the largest of its kind in Asia.

The plan phased out the expansion of academic facilities and extension education for Agriculture, Veterinary Medicine, Animal Sciences, Basic Sciences, Home Sciences, Food Sciences and Technology, Agricultural Engineering and Humanities. The first phase of these was completed in 1977.

Major features of the Master plan are:

Minimum walking distance along shaded pathways to provide shelter from the severe hot weather. Provision for 100% expansion of each constituent college through the reservation of sufficient land. Each building is designed as a system of interlinking courts on a regular structural grid of 7.2 m × 7.2 m; each court forming a basic additive element without creating a sense of incompleteness. To this end, building elements are standardized, economizing on cost and the time for construction. These courtyards also play an important role in moderating the harsh desert climate.

Intensified use of common facilities is shared by the departments. The core of the campus is a Central Plaza with four important buildings, the Nehru Library, the Administrative Building, the Indira Gandhi Auditorium and the Gandhi Bhawan. The Plaza looks into an artificial lake and provides a central meeting place for students, faculty, farmers and general public. The Gandhi Bhawan for extension education and training farmers has a large exhibition hall, museum, studios, workshops and offices; exhibition halls on different levels face open courtyards and are linked by ramps.

The Home Science College, one of the principal buildings in the campus, is a simple load bearing brick structure. It is designed in the form of interconnecting landscaped courtyards.[7]

Abhijeet Ray who worked with JKC in early 70s describes him as, *"He was not a flashy architect. He worked with right proportions. He believed in functions and did not allow any compromise on function."*

J K Chowdhury used to say, "Young man! Fenestration is the most important thing in a building".

He worked with right proportion in both two dimensions and three dimensions. While working out the grid for the Agricultural University, Haryana, J K Chowdhury worked out a system where every building block could have been used for any purpose, thus the time spent in the construction and money spent in the time was reduced. He believed in not to waste any space for any fancy ideas. He believed in conservation of land for future expansion of buildings. Chowdhury had inspired many young architects. He moulded me in his mould, and what I have used in my professional career, the learning came from my experience in JKC office".

[7] Journal of The Indian Institute of Architects, May-June 1995, Volume 60, ISSUE 04, Editor Anil Nagrath, Associate editor Harshad Bhatia, page 7

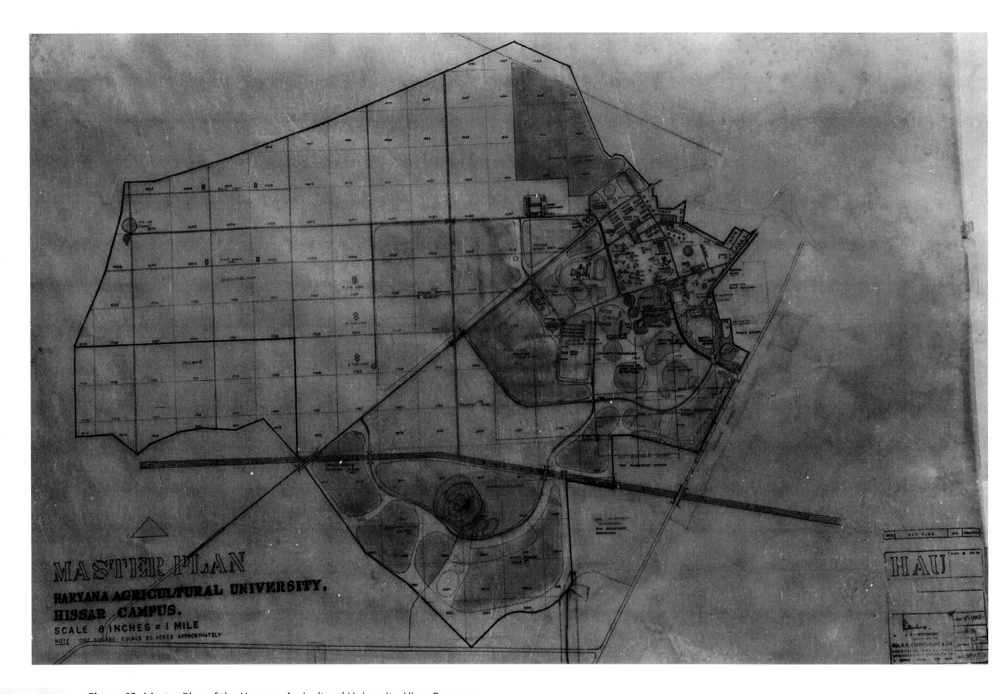

MASTER PLAN

HARYANA AGRICULTURAL UNIVERSITY,
HISSAR CAMPUS.

SCALE 8 INCHES = 1 MILE
NOTE ONE SQUARE EQUALS 25 ACRES APPROXIMATELY

HAU

Figure 42 Master Plan of the Haryana Agricultural University, Hisar Campus

VIEW OF CENTRAL COURT FACING THE UNDERGRADUATE
LECTURE THEATRES AND THE MULTI-STOREYED
POST GRADUATE BLOCK

Figure 43 View of Central Court facing the Undergraduate Lecture Theatres and the Multi-storied Post Graduate Block of Haryana Agricultural University, Hisar

VIEW OF
HOME SCIENCE COURT (B) FACING UNDERGRADUATE
LECTURE THEATRES AND MULTI-STOREYED POST GRADUATE BLOCK

Figure 44 View of Home Science Court facing Undergraduate Lecture Theatres and Multi-Storeyed Post Graduate Block of Haryana Agricultural University, Hisar

VIEW FROM CENTRAL COURT LINKING
HOME SCIENCE COURT (C) AND ENTRANCE COURT

Figure 45 View from Central Court linking Home Science Court and Entrance Court of Haryana Agricultural University, Hisar

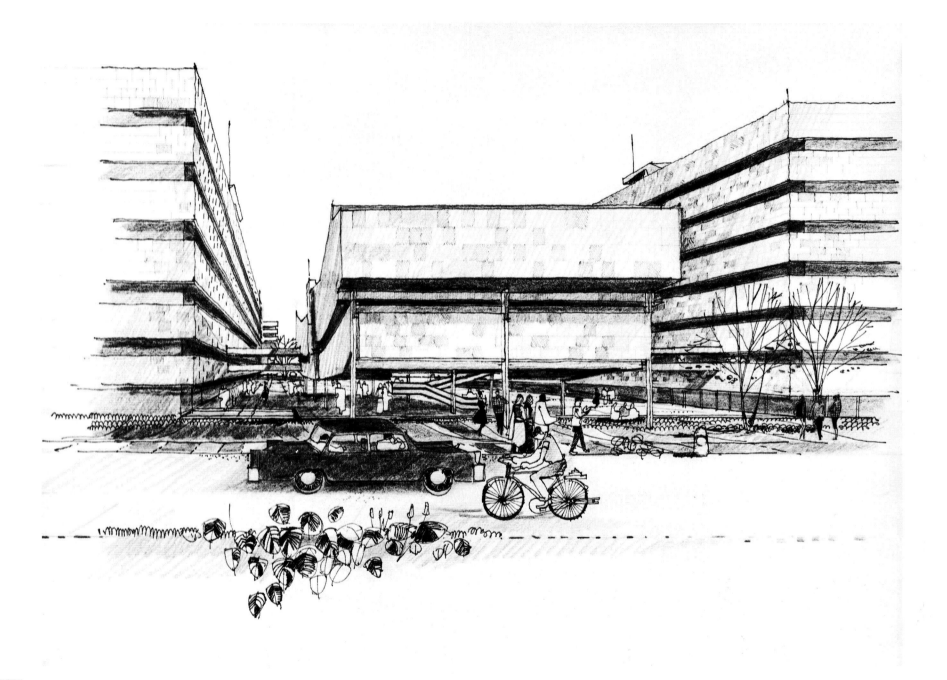

Figure 46 Library Block of Haryana Agricultural University, Hisar

Figure 47 Common activity area of Haryana Agricultural University, Hisar

Figure 48 Haryana
Agricultural University, Hisar
[*Photograph*: Piyush Das]

Figure 49 View through the courtyard of Agricultural University, Hisar

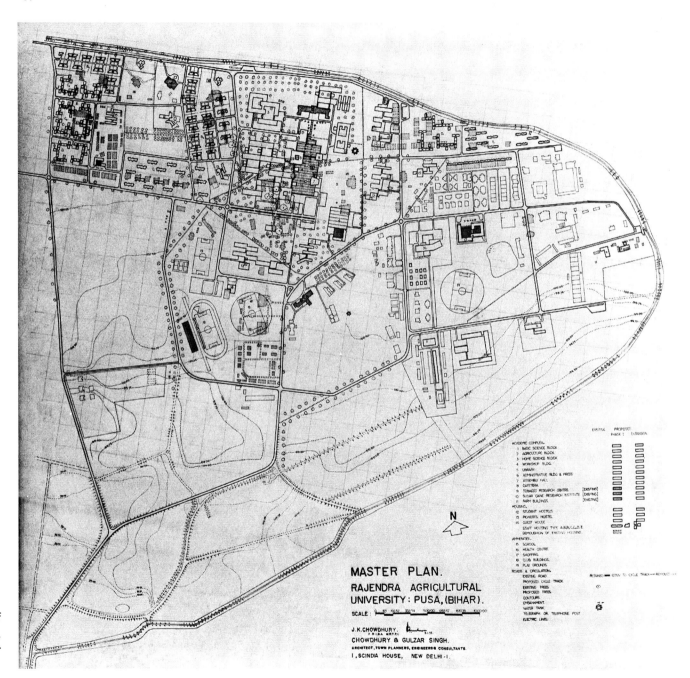

Figure 50 Master Plan of Rajendra Agricultural University, Bihar

Royal Afghan Embassy, New Delhi

Figure 51 Model of Royal
Afghan Embassy, New Delhi

Assam Agricultural University

Figure 52 Master Plan of Assam
Agricultural University

57

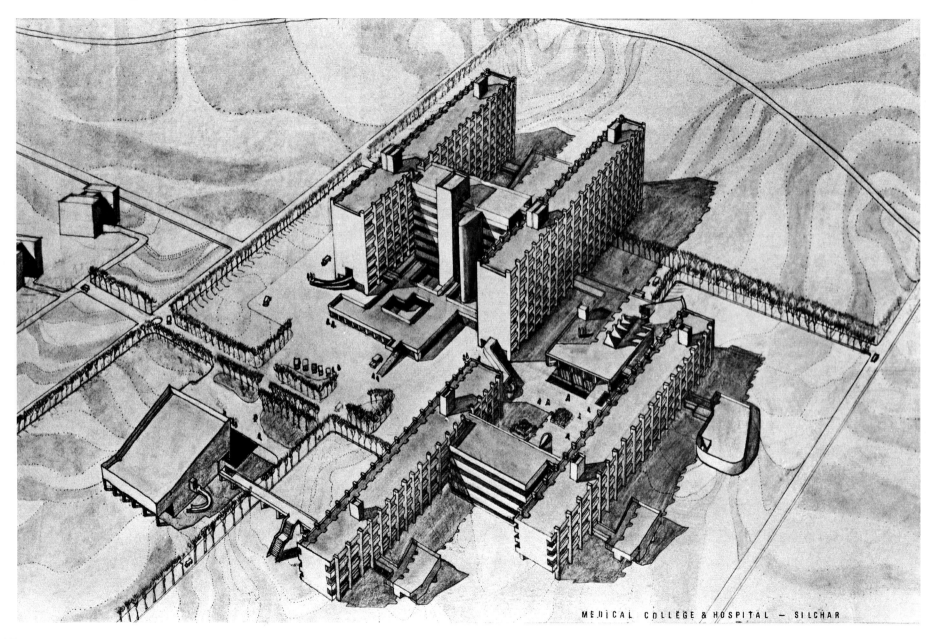

MEDICAL COLLEGE & HOSPITAL — SILCHAR

Figure 53 Map of Medical College and Hospital, Silchar

Medical College and Hospital, Jammu

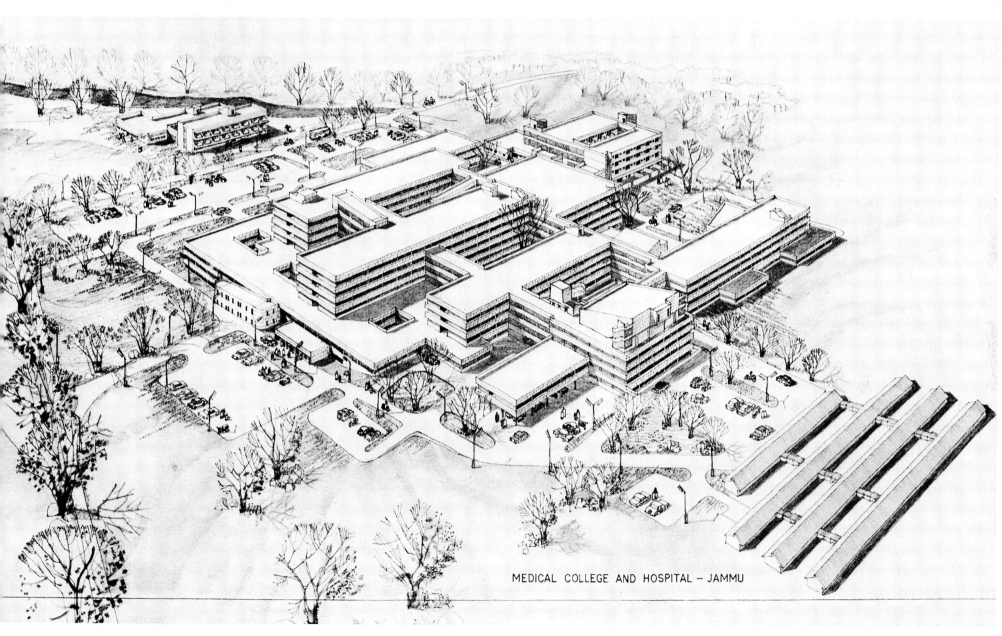

MEDICAL COLLEGE AND HOSPITAL – JAMMU

Figure 54 Map of Medical College and Hospital, Jammu

Medical College, Malda

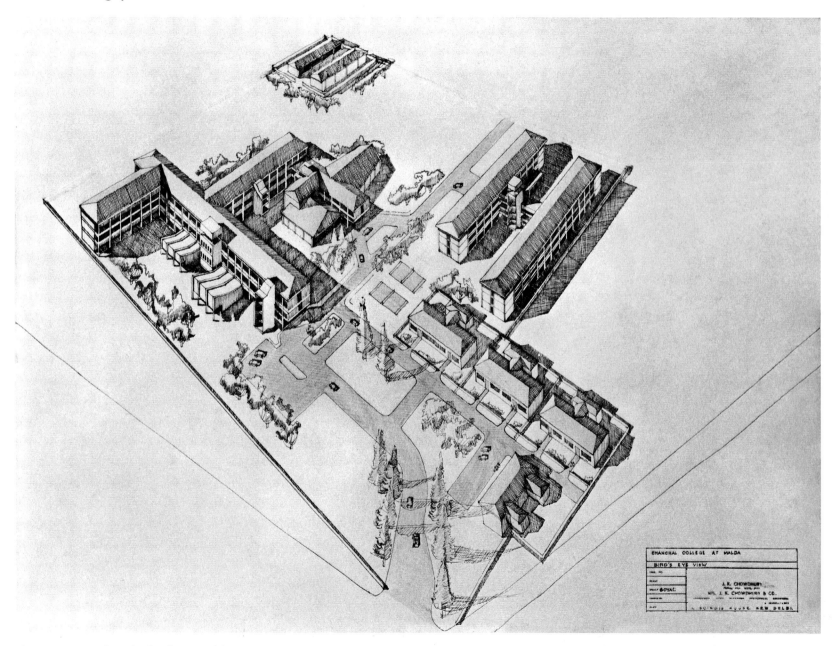

Figure 55 Map of Medical College, Malda

Foreign Post Office Building, New Delhi

Figure 56 Perspective view of Foreign Post Office Building

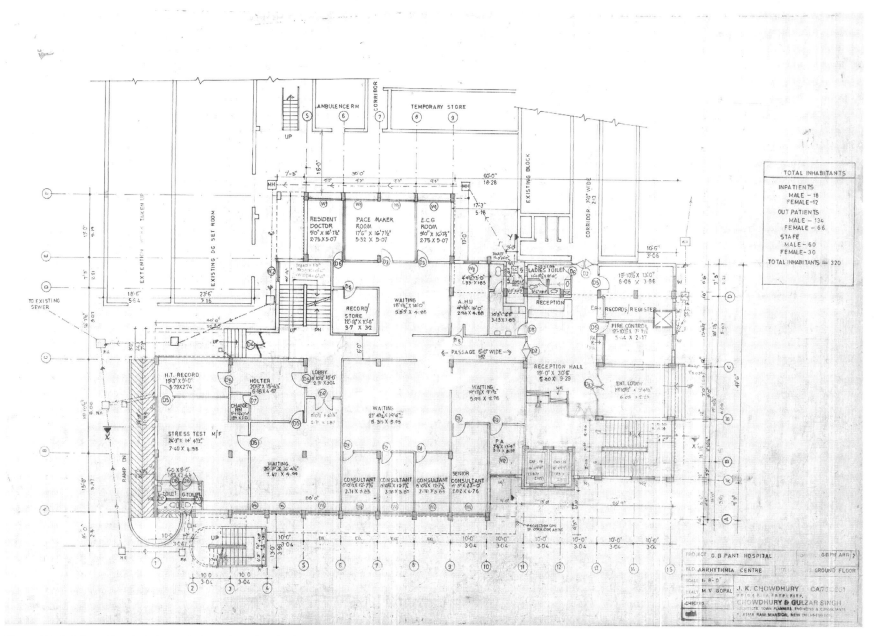

Figure 57 G B Pant Hospital, Ground Floor Plan of Arrhythmia Centre [*Source*: Scanned from the original drawings at Jor Bagh Residence of Jugal Kishore Chowdhury]

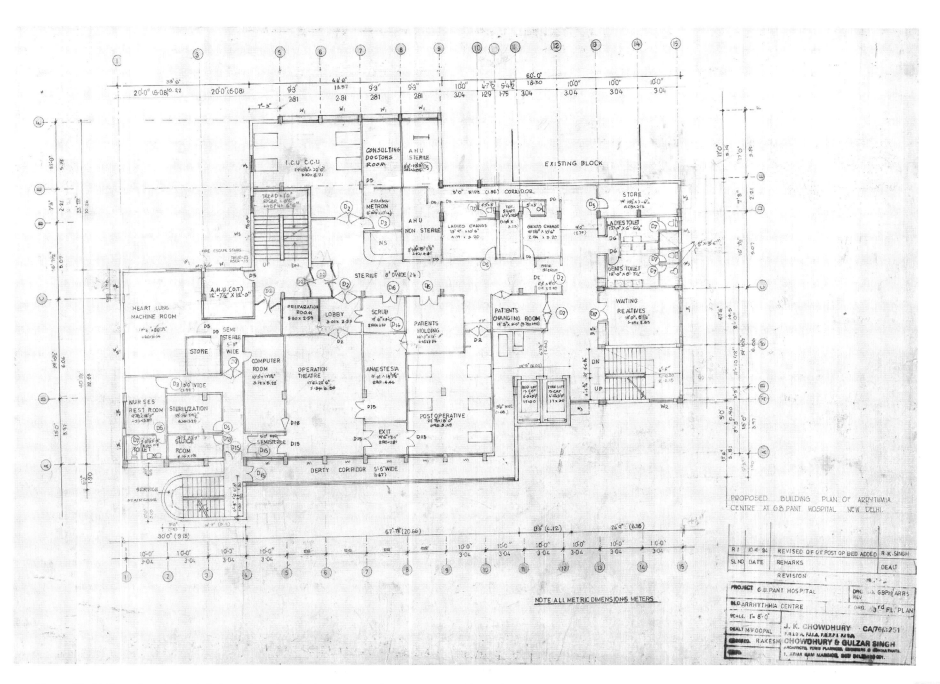

Figure 58 G B Pant Hospital, Third Floor Plan of Arrhythmia Centre [*Source*: Scanned from the original drawings at Jor Bagh Residence of Jugal Kishore Chowdhury]

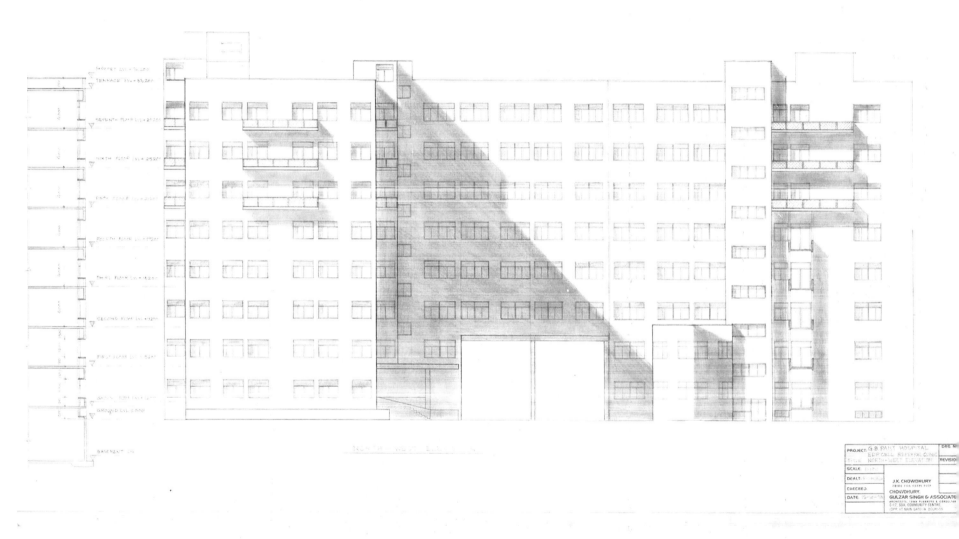

Figure 59 G B Pant Hospital, EPD Cell, North West Elevation [*Source*: Scanned from the original drawings at Jor Bagh Residence of Jugal Kishore Chowdhury]

LNJP Hospital, New Delhi

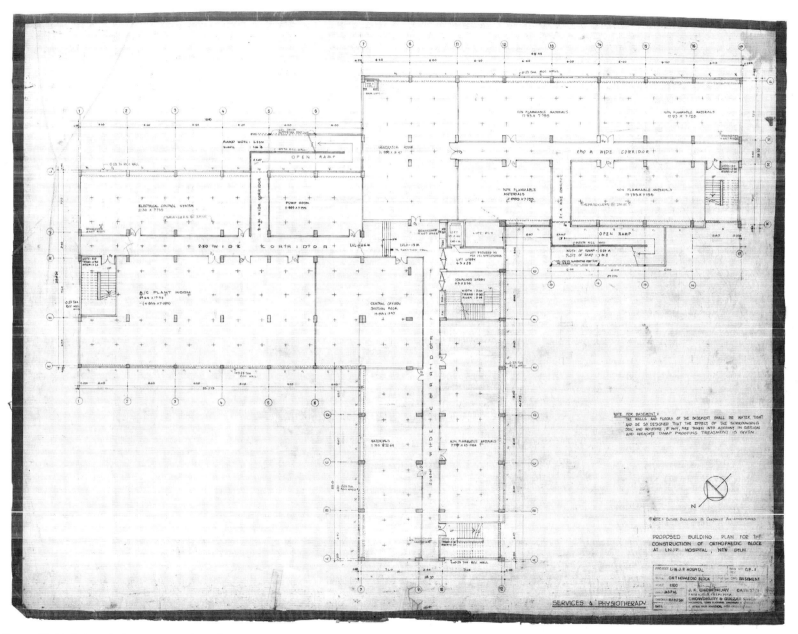

Figure 60 LNJP Hospital, Basement plan of Orthopaedic Block [*Source*: Scanned from the original drawings at Jor Bagh Residence of Jugal Kishore Chowdhury]

University of Jammu

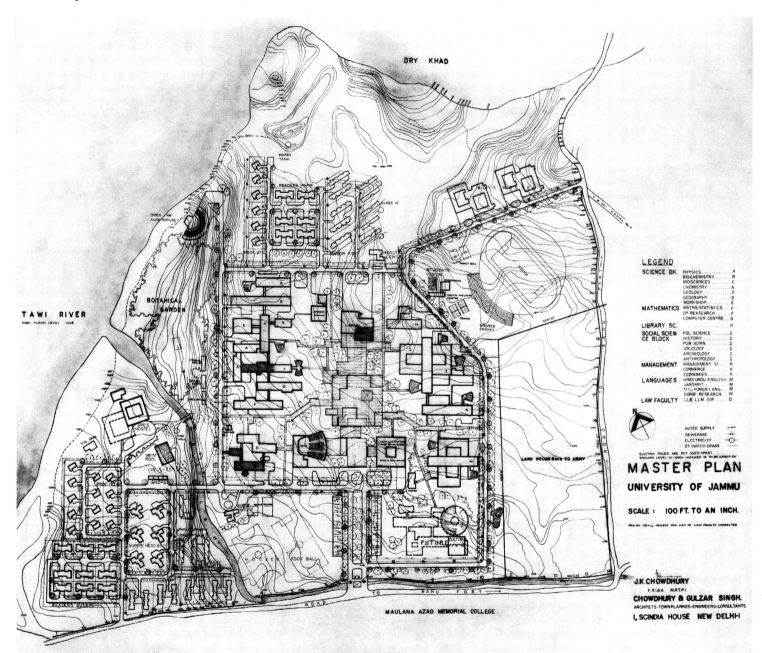

Figure 61 Master Plan for University of Jammu

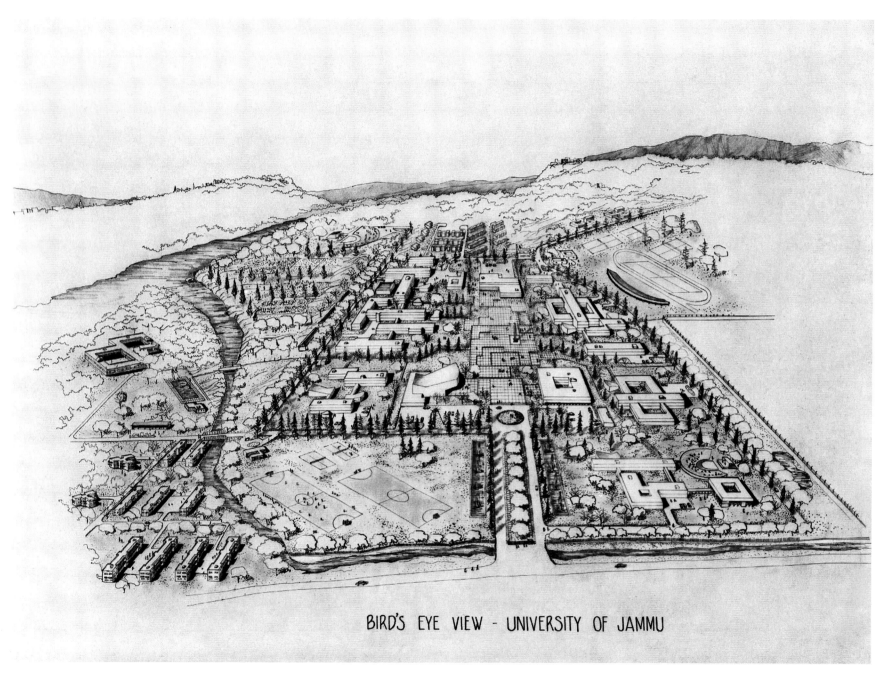

BIRD'S EYE VIEW - UNIVERSITY OF JAMMU

Figure 62 Bird's eye view of University of Jammu

Figure 63 Development Model for University of Jammu

Figure 64 University Column, University of Jammu

VIEW OF THE ENTRANCE COURT

Figure 65 View of the Entrance Court

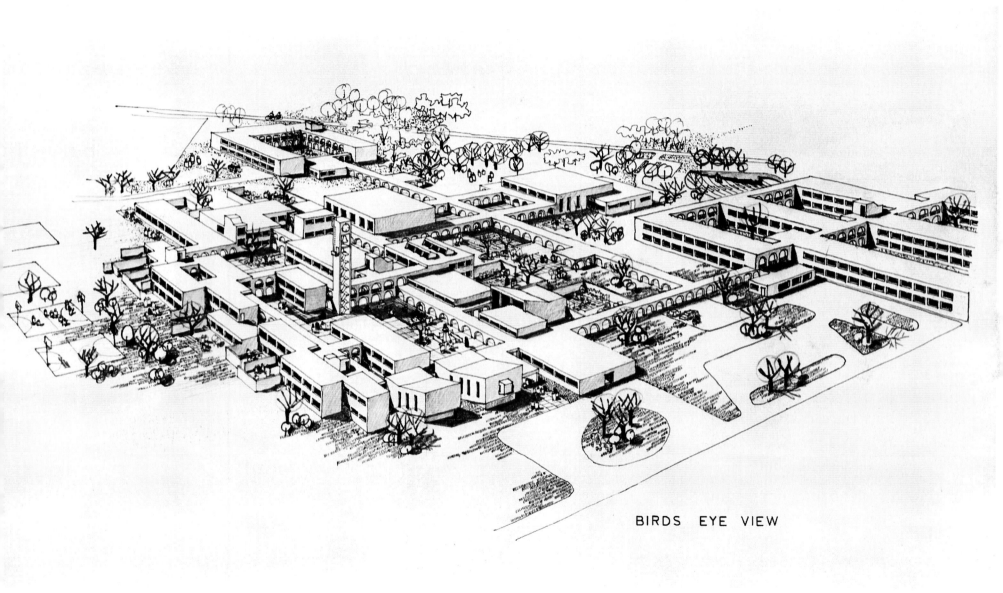

BIRDS EYE VIEW

Figure 66 Bird's eye view

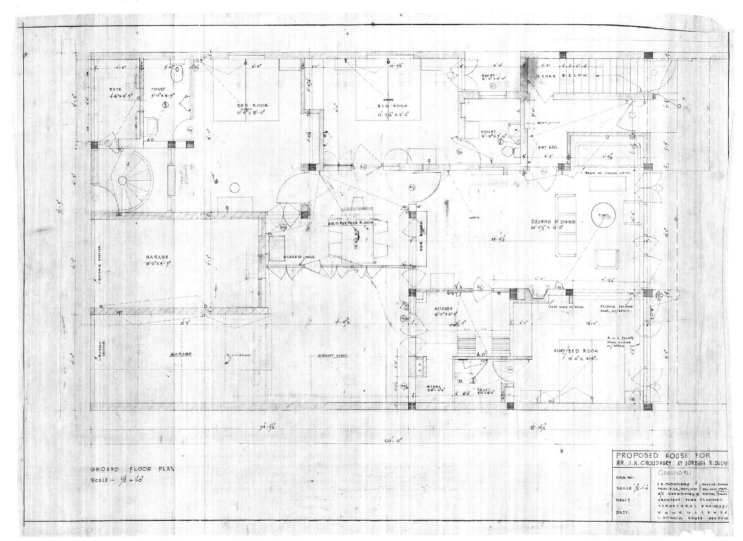

Figure 67 Ground Floor Plan of House at Jor Bagh [*Source*: Scanned from the original drawings at Jor Bagh Residence of Jugal Kishore Chowdhury]

"When I joined him (1970–72), I was a fresher. So I don't think I am at a position to evaluate him as an architect at that time. But I would say, he was very thorough and a tough master. He knew his job very well. He would be in the studio personally and look in to all drawings, every details, every lettering. He cared a lot for the efficiency of the buildings. His designs were very function oriented and he used to achieve great heights of aesthetic through that. He cared about every little detail and he was a master in detailing. He was the perfect architect. In his buildings you can see the sense of system of circulation, touch of aesthetics. The learning I got there has been a treasure for me."

— Shovan K. Shah, Dean, Sharda University

7
Design Ideas, Building Elements

A building is a system of various elements. Starting from there, structural elements to non-structural elements, a building is composed of foundations, walls, fenestrations, structural members, roofing, vertical communication modes (ramps, staircase,) etc. A building can be considered as a living entity with the circulation of light and air.

Jugal Kishore Chowdhury did miracles with all these elements. Whether it was staircase or a window, whether it was a building form or a *jaali*, fulfilling the basic requirements of a building he created these elements with unique innovativeness.

Figure 68 A staircase in IIT Delhi

Form and facade

Figure 69 Form and facade

Allow light, vision, air...

Figure 70 Different *jaalis* allowing light, vision, air

"Young man! Fenestration is the most important element in a building."
– *J.K. Chowdhury*

Figure 71 Different fenestrations

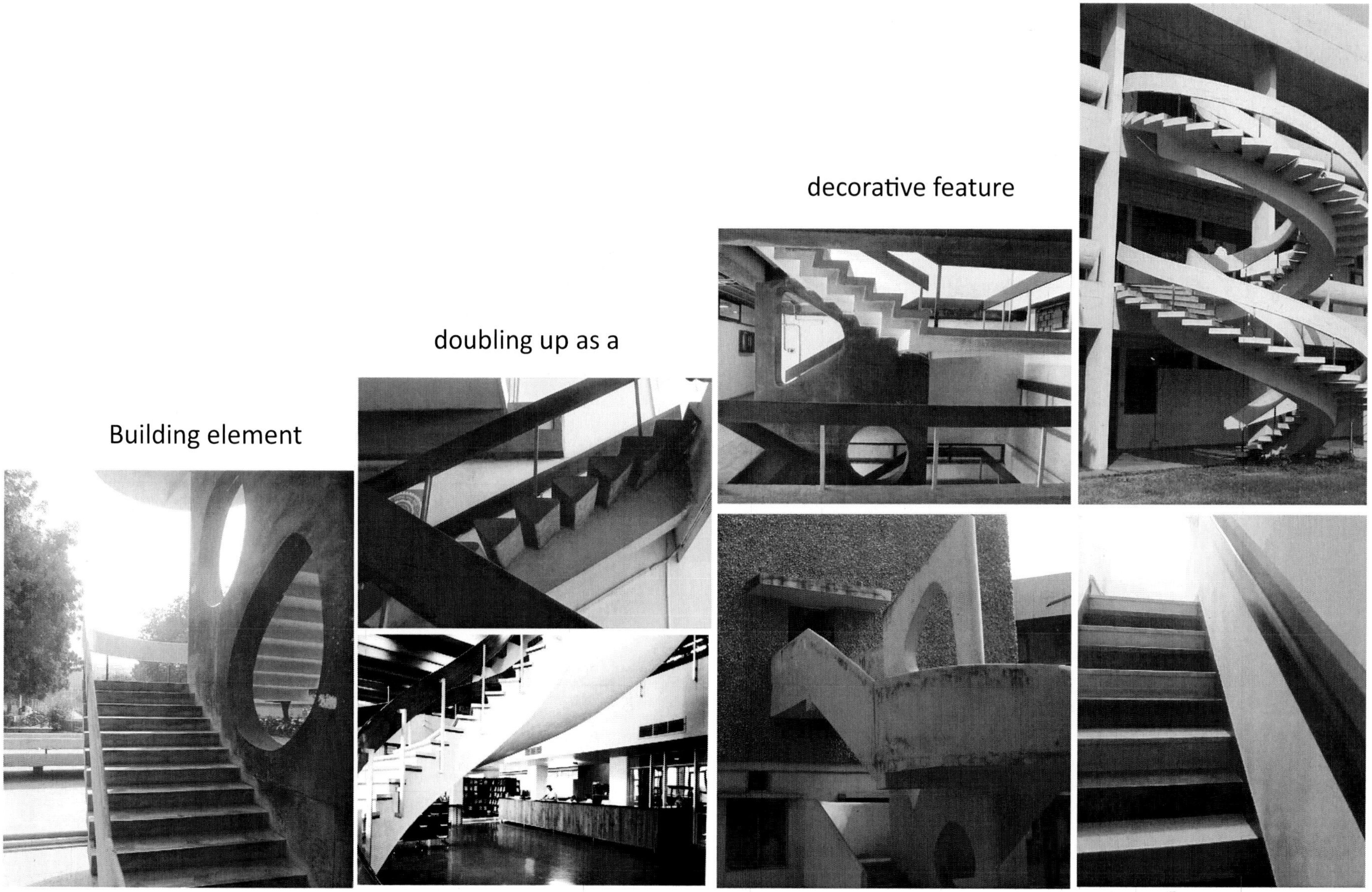

Building element

doubling up as a

decorative feature

Figure 72 Building element doubling up as a decorative feature

8
Master of Details

Figure 73 Staircase at Jor Bagh House designed by JKC [*Photograph*: Piyush Das]

Figure 74 A chair at Jor Bagh house designed by JKC [*Photograph*: Piyush Das]

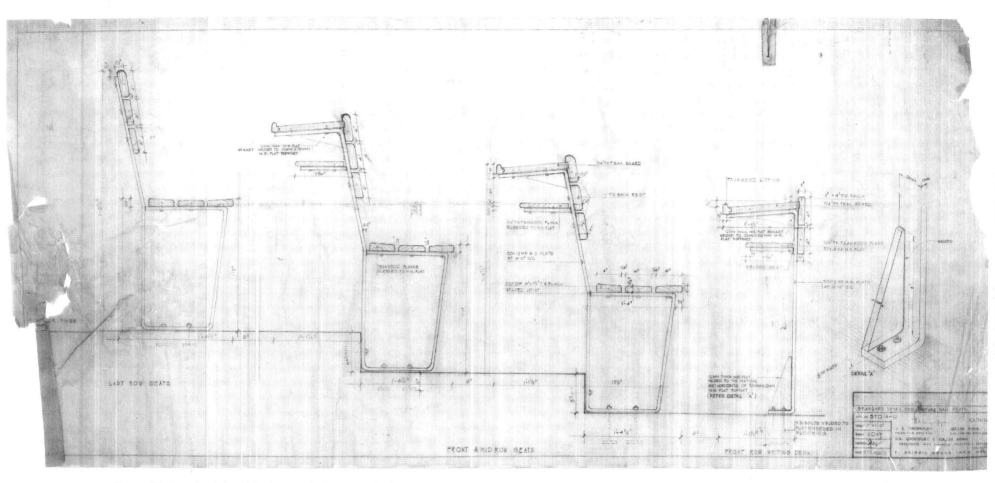

Figure 75 Standard detail for lecture hall seats. Inbuilt storage system is noticeable for the last and middle row seats. Additional writing desk is provided for the front row seats. M.S. members and teak wood are used for the chairs [*Source*: Scanned from the original drawings at Jor Bagh Residence of Jugal Kishore Chowdhury]

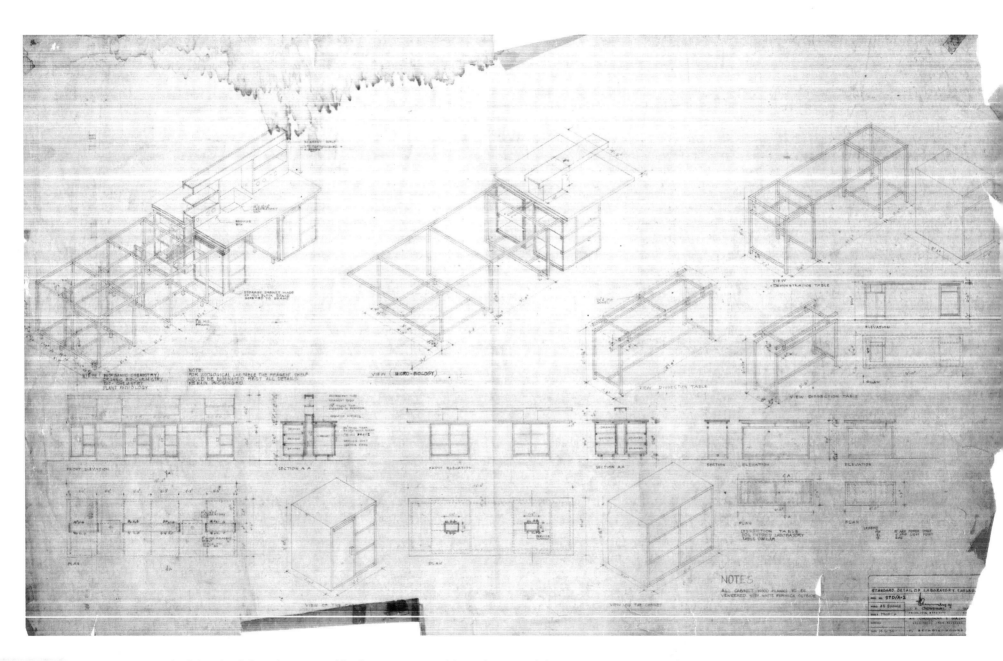

Figure 76 Standard details of the Laboratory tables [*Source*: Scanned from the original drawings at Jor Bagh Residence of Jugal Kishore Chowdhury]

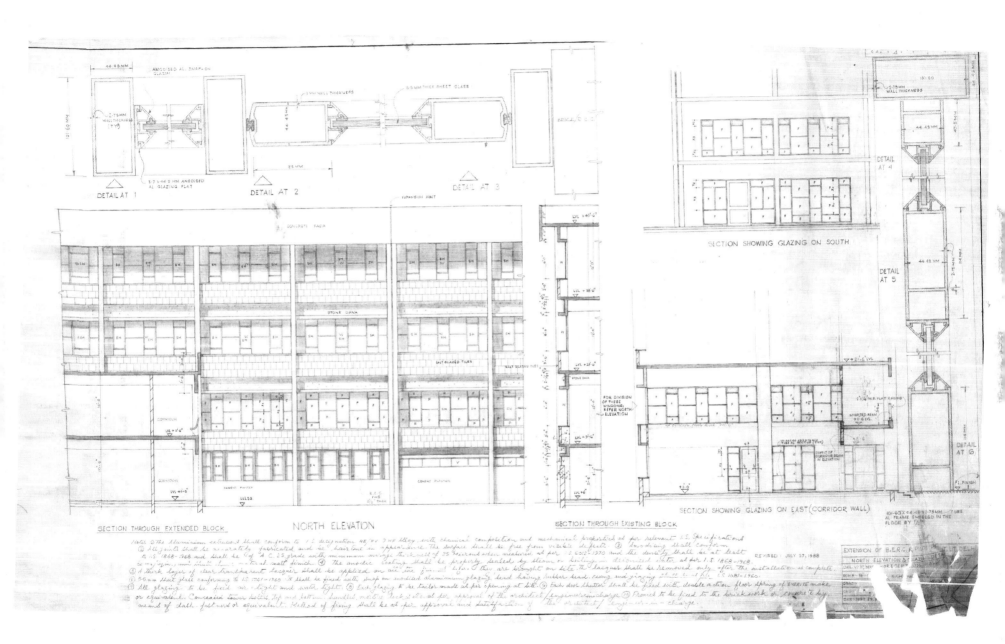

Figure 77 Expansion of IIT Delhi [*Source*: Scanned from the original drawings at Jor Bagh Residence of Jugal Kishore Chowdhury]

9

The Visionary Planner: The Man Who Spoke About Population, Area Development and Sustainability in India in 1964

Shri Chowdhury was a member of the Institute of Town Planners, India, for a number of years, Vice-President during 1963–1964 and twice President during 1964–1965 and 1965–1966. During the first tenure of his presidency, he successfully organized the Thirteenth Annual Town and Country Planning Seminar at Ahmedabad in October 1964. The theme of the seminar was "Industrialization and its Role in Urban and Regional Development." In his presidential address, Shri Chowdhury emphasized the importance of industrial development, especially the large industrial projects which act as foci of regional development. Steel plants and other large industrial projects provided the basis for the development of small and medium industries, new townships, and a whole host of commercial and other activities.[8]

Presidential Address By J.K. Chowdhury: Thirteenth Annual Town and Country Planning Seminar, Ahmedabad: October 1964

We are indeed very fortunate that this year we have been able to hold our annual seminar here in this historic city of Ahmedabad, the capital of the newly born state of Gujarat which is known for its vitality and progressive ideas, its architectural beauty and craftsmanship, its textile industry and exquisite textile designs. It is in this state that there was a real fusion of Muslim and Hindu architecture. Here it reached its highest per action. This is the state which gave birth to the greatest man in India of our generation, Mahatma Gandhi, as well as other great national leaders such as Vallabhbhai Patel and Bhulabhai Desai through whose untiring and selfless efforts and personal sacrifices we have achieved our freedom. We are extremely grateful to the Government of Gujarat and to you, Mr. Chief Minister, for the kind invitation and cordial welcome extended to us to this well-known city and for making all arrangements for our comfort and for providing us with all the facilities for holding this seminar. Our members and delegates have come from all parts of India. They represent central government, state governments, local bodies and many other organizations. It is a very valuable and worthwhile occasion for us to be able to meet, to discuss, to exchange ideas, to profit from each other's experiences and to thrash out differences in formulating united and coordinated plans and policies and to evolve techniques for the creation of a physical environment that will satisfy our material and spiritual needs. Sir, your presence with us this afternoon gives us great hope of success in our debarkations. The fact that you have invited us to Gujarat, to hold this seminar on "Industrialization and its role in urban, rural and regional development" itself proves how deeply interested you are in the 'development of Gujarat and your desire to identify yourselves with the aims and objectives of the Institute of Town Planners. You have dedicated your life to the cause of the country. We know you through your work and the great sacrifices

---

[8] Newsletter ITPI, 2011

you have made in your life for the cause of the common man. You are a great planner yourself. Planning is not a new idea for you. In fact, you are a planner in the real sense, because you deal closely with human beings in all aspects of their problems and understand them much better than many of us. No planning can be successful if the planners ignore the basic needs and problems of human life.

Need for a New Planning Outlook

The development of world events during the past few decades leaves no doubts in our minds that we need to change completely our outlook in planning. A stage has now been reached when we have to think in terms of not only regional and national planning but of overall world planning, because it is becoming increasingly difficult for one country to remain isolated from the problems of another. Today, it is not so much a question old in political ideology or doctrine but a question of the survival of the entire human race. The problem is of food, shelter and employment for all. Therefore, the whole question of planning has to be looked at from a much wider angle now than ever before. If 10–15% of the world population live on diets with insufficient calories, 50% on under-nourished diets and only 33% has adequate food, what will happen when the world population is doubled during the next 35 years from over 3 billion to over 6 billion? Are we in a position even to ensure that our present inadequate rate of food supply will not be further lowered? We talk of improving our health and standard of living for the remaining 65% of the population, the bulk of who are living in regions where the rate of population growth is comparatively high and standards of living very low. The improvement of the economic and social standards of this 65% of the world population will inevitably place a heavy demand on the food supply. It is a matter of great disappointment and concern for all, that in spite of rapid and radical scientific and technological developments in the world today, we have not been able to make much progress in slowing down the abnormal rate of population growth and to ensure adequate supply of food and provide housing and employment for all. There exists a tremendous imbalance in the geographical distribution of world population and world resources. A balance between the two cannot be achieved by any policy of 'expansionism' but only by a 'world understanding' of our mutual problems and needs for supply and demand, conservation and development of resources. The sooner we are able to bring about this understanding, the greater is the hope for survival of the human race. Every nation must play its part effectively to control its population and conserve and develop its resources judiciously and give high priority to facilitate maximum food production and its processing and distribution beyond their political and geographical frontiers.

Planning in India

India with her 440 million population rapidly growing to a figure of 800 million or even more in the next 35 years poses a tremendous challenge to the nation's plans for food, housing and employment. Our Five Year Plans drawn up by economists have been carefully thought outland their aims and objectives are well-defined against heavy odds, progress in several directions has been made and this has helped to strengthen to soothe extent the foundations for building up our economic and social life. Unfortunately, the tempo of development has, not, been able to catch up with the rapidly growing population. The Third Five Year Plan emphasizes a long-term programme for the development of the country's national resources, agricultural and industrial advances and an integrated scheme of regional and national development. We are now on the eve of the formulation of the Fourth Five Year Plan. If we look back and think what we have really achieved in our previous plan periods in the fields of community development, rural and urban housing programmes, slum clearance and urban renewal programmes, we find that we have progressed very little. Very high priority was given in all the preceding plans to the community development programme with the object of increasing agricultural development and improving the economic, social and cultural life of the communities and enormous amounts have been spent in this venture but without much proportionate return. The crux of the problem for slow progress and even failure of the community development programme in many areas does not lie in its concept but perhaps because of its aims and objectives not being identified with those of the Town and Country Planning. Community development forms a part of Town and Country Planning and cannot be isolated from it just as the finger cannot be isolated from the hand. They are inseparable. In the Fourth Five Year Plan we ought to reconsider the urgency of re-organizing the community project organization and merge it with the Town & Country Planning Organization both at the central and state levels, leaving the agricultural extension service and other promotional activities with regard to agriculture and food production to the existing agencies and departments of the state government, or alternatively let the Town and Country Planning be merged with the Community Planning and Housing Organization so that the aims and objectives will be clear and planning will be carried on effectively in co-ordinated and comprehensive manner.

Population and Land Problem

India is a small country if we consider that we have comparatively much less and per head of our population than in Europe, USA or Russia. According to the 1951 census, India had 2+ acre of land per head of our population (or even less as there was a possible error in the census) as against 12.64 acres in USA, 30.46 acres in USSR and 4.27 acres in Europe. In 1961, our land per capita has gone down to 1.7 acres (all land) and only 1.02 acres (usable land). These figures will be further reduced to half when our population is doubled in the course of the next 35 years, i.e. by the year 2000 we shall have only half an acre of usable land or less per head to support our population. Are we sure that India will be able to produce enough food even with intensive cultivation with only half an acre of land per head of our population? This seems impossible. Britain with one acre of land per head (in 1961) with all her efforts of conserving agriculture lands has not been able to make herself self-sufficient in food. India's position seems to be even more critical than that of Britain. A similar situation will arise in the regions of the world where the land population ratio is reaching a critical stage. I have earlier pointed out that if there is no 'world understanding' in respect of conservation, development and distribution of world resources, it is not unlikely that world may explode under the pressure of population. Dr. Raymond Well, an American demographer, predicted that unrelieved famines would occur beginning in 1970, only five years from now, in India, Pakistan and China as he found that to feed the population by that year, the food production has to be raised by 150% 'an impossible target'. The recent food shortage in our country is a pointer to food crisis in the future. From all available facts it is not difficult to surmise that if the rate of food production in all countries is not accelerated, there is every possibility of a world shortage of food. Even if we want to import food from abroad, we may not be able to obtain it.

Urgency for a National Land Use Policy

This immediately leads us to the conclusion that there is great urgency to conserve our land resources and more especially our agricultural land. Britain realized this a few years ago and prepared a land-use map including, among other things, detailed analysis of soil characteristics and introduced the Town and Country Planning Act 1947 whereby every part of land has been brought under development control. In other words, Britain's land for all practical purposes has been nationalized. Considering the critical land–population ratio in our country, it seems imperative to have a definite land-use policy so that misuse of land is curbed without any further delay. On one hand, we are emphasizing the greatest need 'for agricultural development and food production by spending cores of rupees for irrigation, reclamation, soil conservation, etc.,' and on the other hand, everybody has the right to do whatever he likes with his own lands. It is a pathetic sight to see large areas of derelict land, spread all over the country lying waste while agricultural land' is being encroached upon by industrial and urban development. There is no effective legislation to prevent misuse of land. Brick kilns have been sprawling like expanding craters over valuable agricultural land. Extractive industries mining surface and underground, have been misusing land without adequate control. In many cases of extractive industries, minerals are being left underground partially extracted. Land erosion and water-logging are increasing every day. There are scores of other destructive activities which are continually reducing our valuable land everywhere. Anyone who has travelled by air over the country must have noticed the devastated condition of our land on which our future generations will have to live and find their daily bread. In the national interest such a state of affairs cannot be allowed to continue. We need a definite land-use policy to conserve our valuable land.

It is a fallacy that India has plenty of land. This illusion must be removed from the minds of all our people. Once we realize our land position, it will not be difficult for the government to introduce the necessary legislation for judicious control and development of our land. It is true that there are vested interests involved in land and there is the danger of political exploitation; but we hope that our political leaders will keep our national interests above everything else in formulating a uniform land policy in the best interest of the country.

In so far as our rural land is concerned, a directive particularly with regard to its use is immediately necessary and to bring land under the purview of the Town and Country Planning legislation which is now being adopted for comprehensive development in 15 States in India. Scientific control of land use will not be possible immediately till the time we are in a position to obtain an inventory of land resources with full particulars relating to soil characteristics existing land-use pattern, geological, mineral, hydrographical topographical and other data. It is hoped that great emphasis will be laid on the preparation of a proper land-use survey during the Fourth Five Year Plan so that at least in the Fifth Five Year Plan we are in a position to prepare our development plans in a comprehensive manner designating land for its right use. In regard to the urban land, it is necessary to give a general directive to prevent injudicious use of land particularly for housing developments as the present trend is to expand our urban areas in decreasing density, eating into the adjacent valuable agricultural land, thereby not only reducing our good usable agricultural land still further, but also increasing the cost of transportation and other social overheads in urban development. Density control in urban areas, therefore, must be exercised to conserve land.

Housing: A Productive Factor in National Economy

It is now an accepted fact that housing is not a social liability but a positive and productive factor in the development of our national economy, and it is for this reason that housing must be regarded as one of the most important factors constituting the long-term comprehensive development plan and the state must take that responsibility to make it a part of the overall national, social, economic and physical plans and programmes. We, in our previous Five Year Plans, have made very little progress in our housing development programmes. It is learnt that even in the Fourth Five Year Plan which is being formulated now, not much importance has been given to the housing development programme. We hope that serious consideration is given to the question of housing development in the country, as it plays a positive role in the development of our national economy.

The greatest handicap in our urban improvement, slum clearance and housing development has been due to lack of urban land speculation. Experience from other countries has shown that it is almost impossible to improve our urban conditions and provide housing to the people without eliminating land speculation. Many countries have been able to introduce legislation whereby urban land has been municipalized. Considering the magnitude and seriousness of our problem, the first positive step necessary to facilitate housing development in the country is to find out the ways and means to prevent land speculation so that compensation payable for land acquisition in the public interest would not be prohibitive, and implementation of the urban improvement and development programmes becomes feasible to ease the acute housing shortage all over the country.

Inventory of Resources: Prerequisite for Scientific Planning

The National Atlas of India and the techno-economic surveys of various States prepared by the National Council of Applied Economic Research seem to be the only inventories of resources on which are based our national and state plans. But these are far from adequate as they do not give the degree of information and details required for scientific planning. It is, therefore, essential that no time should be lost in the preparation of an inventory of resources of our physical, human and manmade resources. Who should prepare the surveys and collect data for this inventory? I think, States must take the initiative and responsibility under the overall directive of the Centre, assisted by special agencies and regional universities so that during the Fourth Plan a sound foundation is laid for the preparation of all our future Five Year Plans on a more rational and scientific basis, and we can make obligatory for all state governments to prepare comprehensive development plans within the framework of our national plans. An inventory of our resources is the pre-requisite for all scientific planning and, therefore, it ought to be the first step towards the introduction of comprehensive scientific planning for utilization of our physical and human resources.

Need for a Separate Ministry for Town Planning, Housing, Community Development and Local-Self Government

At present, the Town and Country Planning is the responsibility of the Ministry of Health; Housing of the Ministry of Works; and Community Development of the Ministry of Community Development & Co-operation with the result, co-ordination between Town Planning and Housing and Community Development has not been effective. It is not that the Ministry of Health necessarily be concerned with Town and Country Planning. There is also not much advantage in having Housing with the Ministry of Works. We have been noticing that as a result of separating Town and Country Planning from Housing, housing development all over the country has been going in a piece-meal manner pulling as it were in two different directions. To achieve greater degree of co-ordination between Town Planning and Housing they must be under one Ministry. Similarly, as the aims and objectives of Community Development are the same as those of Town and Country Planning, it is essential that both these organizations should be merged now into each other. Again, as Community Planning or Town Planning is primarily the responsibility of the States and local bodies, it is desirable that the local self-government should also be in the same Ministry both at the Centre as well as in the States so that there is effective coordination.

Figure 78 Group photograph taken on the occasion of the 13th Annual Town and Country Planning Seminar held at Ahmedabad in October 1964

Regional Planning: Only Sound Basis for Planning

The history development of Town and Country Planning in Britain is an illuminating example for all planners. The British realized that physical planning and economic planning are inseparable. They must go hand in hand, as one is an integral part of the other. It is utterly meaningless to prepare a physical plan without considering the economic and social aspects of the community. Similarly, it is equally fruitless to prepare an economic plan without considering its effects on physical development. Regional planning takes into account physical, economic and social aspects of planning, covering a large identifiable area of common interests. It seeks to determine the real characteristics of the area through interlocking of facts of small components by research and analytical studies till full facts are woven into a recognizable pattern of cohesive development looked at from the state and national levels. Though in reality, the ideal region cannot be confined within the limits of political and administrative boundaries, yet for practical reasons the States ought to set up their planning machinery at the district level as well as at the State level so that for the time being the planning functions are restricted within the existing political and administrative boundaries until experience proves necessary to reorganize them. Overall coordinating functions for the district plans should naturally be in the hands of the State Planning Organization which needs to be reorganized with much greater powers of coordination in all planning and development activities of the State to make it effective. The implementation of plans ought to be carried on through the Local Bodies such as the Local Boards, Municipal Village Panchayats, etc. so as to obtain the maximum participation of the people. The plans, however, have to be kept flexible enough to make such adjustments as will be necessary depending on the local conditions.

In addition to State Planning there ought to be Inter-State Regions and Special Regions to be set up for solving Inter-State problems and special area problems with a view to removing regional imbalance. Power to co-ordinate Inter-Slate and Special Regions ought to be vested in the President of India through a Special Act of the Parliament.

Need For Planners and Planning Administrators

Earlier, I have mentioned that comprehensive Town and Country Planning legislation is being enacted by 15 States in India. Introduction of this legislation in the States will be a great leap forward in the right direction in the development of our urban and rural settlements, industrial location and industrial development. We are very happy that the newly born State of Gujarat is also introducing this Act very shortly which will be called the Gujarat Town and Country Planning Act, 1964. We congratulate the Government of Gujarat for the foresight and wisdom of their having taken this important decision. I may, however, mention that both in the planning as well as in the implementation stage the services of a large number of qualified town planners will be necessary. Immediate steps therefore will have to be taken to train not only planners and planning technicians but also planning officials and administrators to take up this responsibility.

In a heavily populated country like India where planning is a vital necessity, we have until now only three planning schools which train about 20–25 town planners in the country annually. This only goes to prove that planning education in the country has been sadly neglected. At the moment, the local authorities are carrying on their planning mostly through nonprofessional planners. There are about 110 town planners in the country: out of whom majority work with government planning departments.

A few who are in private practice as consultants are not even fully occupied with planning work. This is due to the fact that the role of the town planner is not fully understood by the public as yet. But, if proper incentive is not given to the private town planners to utilize their planning experience, it will be difficult for the government to attract people of high calibre to enter the profession. The demand for town planners and planning officials will be increased many times over as soon as comprehensive Town and Country Planning legislation is introduced in all the States. To meet this sudden demand, the government ought to set up immediately at least one Planning School in each State or the universities must take the initiative to impart Planning Education so that every year we should be able to produce at least 1,000 town planners in the country.

Location of Industry and Future Settlement Pattern

India's settlement structure of the future, both urban and rural, will largely depend on the strategy of planning and policy followed in the Fourth Five Year Plan which is now under preparation. However, taking into consideration the present and future land population ratios of our country mentioned earlier, the vital role that industry and industrial location will play in the settlement pattern and re-distribution of our population will not be difficult for us to visualize, once we realize that before the end of the present century only about 20% to 25% of our total population can be supported by agricultural employment and the remaining 75% to 80% will have to be absorbed in non-agricultural sector.

In our Five Year Plans certain broad directive principles and policies regarding "Balanced Industrial Development" have been indicated; but in actual practice, very little have been achieved. The States which are primarily responsible for the development of industries have not been able to organize themselves to establish a proper scientific base for industrial planning and development, relating to their needs, population and resources. For this reason, industrial development has been taking place in a haphazard manner with its consequent ill-effects on the social structure of our cities, especially in some of the industrial cities. If the industrial population of a city is not balanced with the other working population residing in it, socioeconomic imbalance is inevitable. In the expansion or re-development of our towns and cities, particularly industrial cities, this factor should not be lost height of.

Economics of industrial location and settlement of our communities can be studied only through a systematic study and analysis. A proper 'Inventory' of socio-economic and physical surveys of our towns, cities and villages is urgently needed. The Department of Industries, in the State Government, concerned with industries has to play a much greater and responsible role than ever before in the development of industries in the State. Reorganization of this department is an immediate necessity.

In concluding my speech I must add that planning is a highly complex process. To comprehend it in all its aspects needs a very wide range of knowledge and experience. Each country has to evolve its own planning system and development strategy, depending on its own problems and according to its own genius. The experience of other countries helps to make us think in relation to the problems of our own but it does not necessarily solve them. In my speech I have laid great emphasis on scientific land use planning as the basis for all our planning activities. While doing so, I am quite conscious of the political, administrative and technical aspects of land control. In a democracy such as ours, we shall need public support in our land control and development policy but, as I have faith in the people, I do not anticipate any difficulty in following the right path. I have also emphasized the need for reorganization of our existing government machinery concerned with planning problems because I believe that the degree of success to make planning effective will depend to a large extent on how well organized is our administration. I do not for a moment ignore the fact that ultimately the key to the success of all planning and development is effective co-ordination at all level of administration. But co-ordination is an attitude of mind. This attitude can come only if there is clear understanding of our problems and there is an urge to co-operate. Therefore, the success or failure of our planning and development will rest on the co-operation and participation of the people.

Now, I must thank you, Ladies and Gentlemen, for the patient hearing you have given to my address and request the Hon'ble Chief Minister Balwantrai Mehta to inaugurate the Seminar and wish us well in making it a success.

Figure 79 Institute of Town Planners India, Annual Meeting 1966

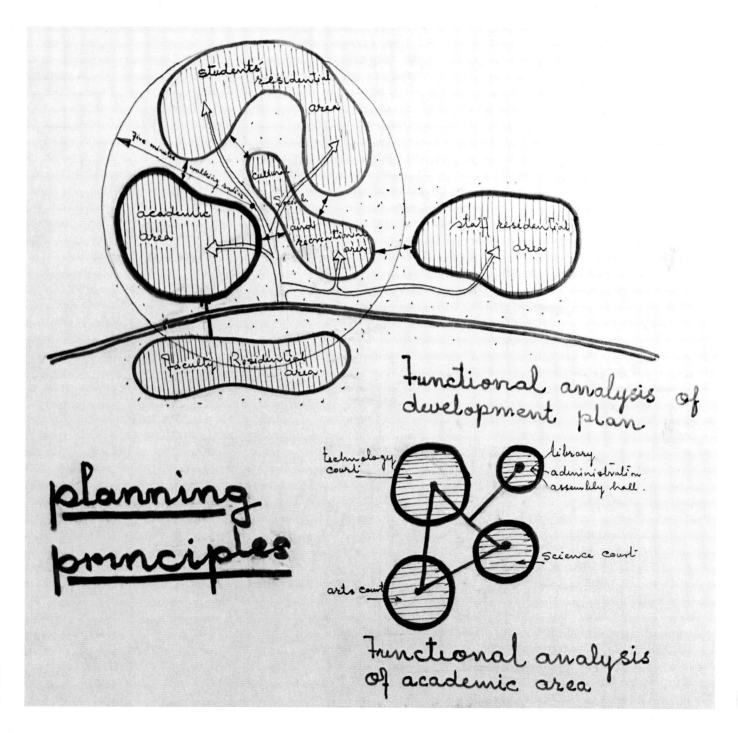

Figure 80 Concept planning for institutional campus

91

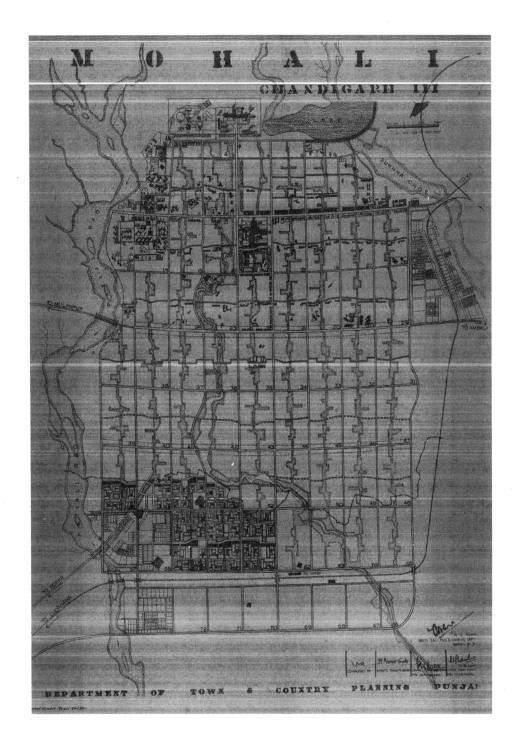

Figure 81 Mohali, Chandigarh III Plan
[*Source*: Scanned from the original drawings at
Jor Bagh Residence of Jugal Kishore Chowdhury]

Master plan for Saraidhella Township

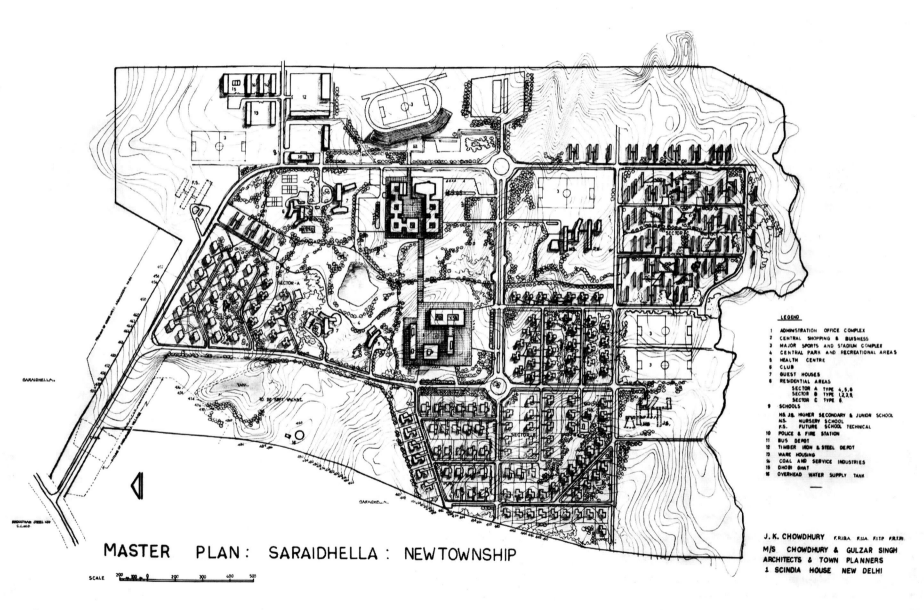

LEGEND

1 ADMINISTRATION OFFICE COMPLEX
2 CENTRAL SHOPPING & BUSINESS
3 MAJOR SPORTS AND STADIUM COMPLEX
4 CENTRAL PARK AND RECREATIONAL AREAS
5 HEALTH CENTRE
6 CLUB
7 GUEST HOUSES
8 RESIDENTIAL AREAS
    SECTOR A TYPE 4,5,8
    SECTOR B TYPE 1,2,3,8
    SECTOR C TYPE 6
9 SCHOOLS
    H.S. J.S. HIGHER SECONDARY & JUNIOR SCHOOL
    N.S. NURSERY SCHOOL
    F.S. FUTURE SCHOOL TECHNICAL
10 POLICE & FIRE STATION
11 BUS DEPOT
12 TIMBER IRON & STEEL DEPOT
13 WARE HOUSING
14 COAL AND SERVICE INDUSTRIES
15 DHOBI GHAT
16 OVERHEAD WATER SUPPLY TANK

J. K. CHOWDHURY F.R.I.B.A. F.I.I.A. F.I.T.P. F.R.T.PI.
M/S CHOWDHURY & GULZAR SINGH
ARCHITECTS & TOWN PLANNERS
1 SCINDIA HOUSE NEW DELHI

MASTER PLAN : SARAIDHELLA : NEW TOWNSHIP

SCALE 200 100 0   200   300   400   500

Figure 82 Master Plan of Saraidhella Township

93

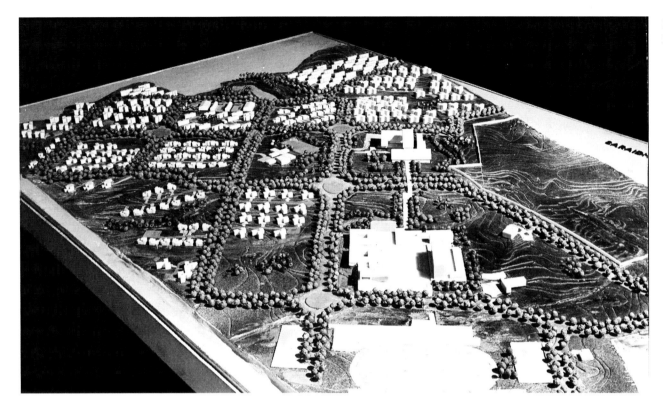

Figure 83 Physical Model for Saraidhella Township

Figure 84 Bird's eye view of Headquarters Administrative Building: Bharat Coking Coal Limited, Saraidhella

10
A Guide and A Mentor

As a visiting professor to the School of Planning and Architecture, New Delhi, J K Chowdhury taught Urban Design and guided thesis of many students. He was closely involved with education and examinations of several universities.

"As a student of his in 1989 I learned that there is no scope for short cuts in Architecture and more so in the practice of the profession. He was a good mentor and always tried to understand the perception of his students and guided us accordingly. He made us understand the subject in greater detail and shared his personal experiences with us to make us understand the requirements of the project. I had done my thesis on the subject "International Convention Centre at Agra" under his guidance. While I was doing my case studies I had shortlisted Vigyan Bhawan and Ashoka Hotel convention centre for the study. He told me that these hardly qualify as convention centres. He told me to do some library study. In spite of my best efforts I failed to locate a similar case study in the vast library of the School of Planning and Architecture. He therefore called me every Saturday to his house at Jor Bagh and made me study there under his personal supervision. He believed in working on construction details of each part of the project. He always laid special emphasis on the design of staircases and windows of the building. He taught us about working on details and circulation systems in planning of spaces, these teaching of his are so true even in the today's scenario.

He made me work at his studio for long hours and spent a lot of time in making clear to me the concepts in Architectural Design and teaching me construction details.

He always insisted on working on details and adopted straight line structures only for the purpose and function, curved elements were used in façade, staircases and fenestration elements. He never believed in doing something only for the sake of doing it and creating something in the name of Architecture which will serve no purpose. He was a man with style as a Person.

After graduation when I wanted to start my own design practice he advised me to go for higher studies and also offered me to document his work but due to personal family reasons I told him, "Sir I will not be able to do so at this point in time and I will have to start my own practice and do whatever little work I have in hand." He then gave me a detailed session on professional practice including how to deal with professional work, what fee should be charged. He also warned be not to adopt any short cuts even while doing complementary jobs for my near and dear ones. He always believed that the way we do or deal with our work reflects in our work culture and the kind of Architecture we create. An architect works in a team as a leader of the concept with a Vision, Concept and Creativity. To deliver the job, he must take the help of all related professionals such as structural designers, engineers, landscape architects, etc. Even if the job is small the importance of every one in creating/realizing the dream of the architect can't be undermined.

— Vijay Garg

As one of the best campus designer in the country, when J. K. Chowdhury guided Parbir Halder in 1990 for his thesis in SPA Delhi, Halder had to say a lot about the experience. He says, *"J. K. Chowdhury was a very logical teacher and had an eye for detailing. He used to understand the level of each student and then guided them accordingly. I found him as an excellent mentor."* After all these years when Halder himself is now designing a music university, he recalls all his learning from the thesis period from J. K. Chowdhury when he helped him to design an Open University in his thesis. The logical approach to any design problem, was something as Halder describes, *"Approach that I learned, I am still using the inferences of them and it turned out to be very productive".*

— Parbir Halder

"I am happy to hear that Sushant is celebrating and holding an exhibition of J K Chowdhury's works. I had the privilege to work with him for nearly 3 years between 1986 and 1989. He was an extraordinary person. I learnt more from him than anywhere else. He was a mentor. Of course IIT Delhi was his most significant project. Within the campus he designed 8-storey residential flat buildings which I helped him document. While a tough master, but he was tender at heart.

He designed many buildings. Off my head, Yogavendra Public School Chandigarh, Arrhythmia Centre and lots more. At the time all drawings in his (J K Chowdhury's) office were made in pencil. One day he came to my desk, pulled my blunt pencil away from my hand and threw it away. He pulled out a sharpened pencil from his pocket and said: "A pencil point is the index of mind. Sharper the pencil, sharper the mind."

— Rajeev Maini

"In 1987, J K Chowdhury took part in a design competition for a fantastic project of a cluster of cities proposed to be built on the exhausted mines and hollowed trenches in vast region in the coal mine belt of Bihar. He worked from the Scindia House office in CP with a team of two people specially hired for this, separate from the regular staff in the office. Three men toiled intensely for 10 days, often late into the evening. The regional scale concept was developed with number of urban centres in an extensive network. Various colourful diagrams and vision sketches were drawn up. Policies were written down. The largest drawing was the entire regional plan with towns and other centres, connecting roads and natural features.

This was laid out on the long table finally to make the most important drawing at one end. A large clear plate was held vertically in front of him. It was kept standing near the edge of the table with the top end tilting away to give it a lean. Through this the plan was visible. The master carefully moved a black pen held in his sharp, thin and steady fingers, to trace on the glass the lines of the in perspective. Adjusting the vanishing points regularly. The grand bird's eye perspectives view emerged on the glass. The reports were given last touches. The submission was finally ready but time was a bit tight that night.

On the eleventh morning at the Gariahat crossing in south Calcutta, a middle-aged lady who was on her way back from a shopping trip to the grocery, all of a sudden found her young son who lived in Delhi, popping out of an Airport Bus slinging a tube of drawings and a large packet without any prior notice.

The previous night in Delhi those two assistants were scolded by the boss for delaying work. But the boss knew he was no less engrossed in the fun of creation for a few days. J K ordered and arranged for and allowed one of the two people to take the earliest flight in the morning to reach the Coal India Headquarters in order to meet the deadline. Thanks to J K indeed. In those days I could never have afforded such a luxurious hometown travel. JKC's face had faded out of memory but his hands and the view, I remember.

— Rajat Ray

"During my Thesis semester (fall of 1989) J. K. Chowdhury was assigned to me and several others as guide. Most of us used to visit his office in Connaught place for our crits. I would describe his personality as kind, a good listener and measured in response. He would not shy away from grabbing the pencil and drawing over your work and then point out vistas, axis, and central artery. When worried about passing he told me, don't worry, you listen to my suggestions. He did care."

— Jitender Vats

11

In Response to IIA Baburao Mhatre Gold Medal: Jugal Kishore Chowdhury

I am grateful to the Indian Institute of Architects for conferring on me the prestigious Baburao Mhatre Gold Medal for the year 1994. It was indeed a pleasant surprise to me when I received the news. That the Institute had appreciated my work and in recognition conferred on me this honour, I am indeed very happy. For architecture truly reflects one's mind and spirit. It reveals one's inner self and culture of the society he belongs to. At the same tune, it makes me think, how deep rooted is my architecture to Indian tradition, art and culture. I believe if architecture is to be a living art, then it must continuously change with the times. Each country has its own deep-rooted culture. Therefore, I believe each country's culture should reflect on its architecture to give its identity. Otherwise, the world will be monotonous to live in. Therefore, I think cultural identity in architecture is perhaps necessary. And if it is so, should it be a conscious attempt of an architect to reflect culture on his work or should it express itself spontaneously in his work, because he himself is a product of the society he belongs to? In my view, architect's work ought to reveal the culture of his time spontaneously if he is true to himself and does not have to work under the pressure or influence of his clients.

I think I am very lucky that no clients of mine, in my fifty years of professional work, tried to influence me in my architectural work. I was left free to design buildings according to my own ideas.

Art or architecture cannot flourish if the clients do not give freedom to an architect to design buildings. Client's appreciation of art and architecture and their patronage is necessary for the development of good architecture. Take the example of Chandigarh, India's first Prime Minister, Nehru, invited one of the world's top architect Le Corbusier and gave him full freedom to plan Chandigarh and design some of the important buildings in Chandigarh not only to express democratic ideals of free India but also to stimulate the younger generation of Indian architects to produce architecture suited for the country. Many intellectuals and pseudo-intellectuals thought that Corbusier's designs were not suitable for our climate and culture. Many others, however, thought it to be good and stimulating. But the fact that Nehru recognized that the architect must be free to design and democracy must uphold the dignity of an artist or an architect was of great significance and something to be remembered and emulated. That Art must grow in freedom is essential.

Our society has to recognize this. We have seen the work of art and architecture during dictatorship and autocratic rules. Even now, we are seeing many such examples in our country and their poor results. Our intelligentsia must wake up to this danger. Otherwise, the country will not be able to progress.

But, freedom does not mean license to do whatever one likes. An Architect must have social responsibility. Architecture is a time-honoured profession that offers service to people and the society. It is not business, motivated by profit. An Architect gets his fees or remuneration for his services commensurate with his labour and time. An Architect like an artist gets his satisfaction from his work which needs dedication and self-involvement. An Architect's satisfaction is more out of his intellectual and emotional involvement. Therefore, the service that he gives is of a personal nature. When a client entrusts a certain building to him for design and construction, the architect must assume full responsibility, not only to produce a real work of art but also execute the project within the cost estimate approved by his client and within certain time frame agreed upon. If the architect fails to keep his commitment, he must be prepared to compensate his for his lapses. Unfortunately, very few architects in India undertake to assume this responsibility. In advanced countries, where an architect is given the license to practice, he accepts full liability. And to do so, he covers his liabilities with an insurance policy. I think it is a high time that we should make it obligatory for an architect to take similar responsibility to restore public confidence.

Unfortunately, the Council of Architecture, which has taken the responsibility of giving a license to practice without adequate training and experience to a young architect soon after completing his academic studies. The Indian Institute of Architects should come forward to 'take full responsibility' of Architectural Education and Training. The Institute should also conduct a 'License Test Examination' after the student gets thorough training and experience for at least a minimum period of 3 years before he is eligible to appear in the 'License Test Exam'. Issue of 'License' to practice may be entrusted to the Council of Architecture which may register the names of such licensed architects and exercise control over them to see that they do not violate the rules and regulations prescribed by the Indian Institute of Architects. Any irregularities committed by the Licensed Architect should be reported to the Institute for taking disciplinary action as per the rules prescribed by the Institute. The Institute should also be responsible to recognize the architectural courses taught in the various educational institutes in the country according to the professional standard to be adopted by the Institute. It is also important that the Institute should conduct all architectural competitions in the country as we have opened The Institute's Chapters in almost all States. At present all these responsibilities have been taken by the Council of Architecture, but it has failed miserably to safeguard the interest of the profession. The Indian Institute of Architects is the only professional body in the country which is competent to look after the profession adequately. The Council of Architecture Act, 1972, must therefore, be changed without any further delay and it should be made obligatory for all architects whether in service or in professional practice to be the members of the Indian Institute of Architects.

In a democracy, the architect's role in the society is becoming highly complex and difficult. It is more so, in a developing country like ours, where the population is still growing rapidly, making land–population ratio critically high and urbanization with industrialization bringing tremendous pressure on land, housing and infrastructure. An architect's responsibility to solve the problems has increased manifold.

They are expected to work with other specialists, in many different fields of planning and development. Introduction of 73rd and 74th Constitutional Amendments Act 1992 strengthens the hand of District Officials, Block Development Officers, Gram Panchayats and Zilla Parishads to make it obligatory to prepare Development Plans with effective coordination at all levels so that the fruits of development can reach the grassroots of our rural communities. This has thrown up a new challenge to the architects and physical planners. Familiar with multi-disciplinary approach to planning and development, they can make themselves very useful in the preparation and development of plans.

The traditional method followed so far has been so slow that development is overtaking planning. Can we blame the people for this? People do not have unlimited patience to wait. To get the approval of a plan alone, from a Local Authority in Delhi, it takes six months to a year or even more and that too after several visits, discussions and persuasions from peon onwards. The corruption level has reached such an unprecedented level that one gets disgusted and demoralized not only in the building departments, but also the rot has taken place in each and every department of the government. The solution lies only with our policy makers and not with architects because architecture and politics do not go together. Planning is dictated by the social and political forces that are working. An architect working as a planner cannot however be isolated from the social and community activities. In fact, he should work as an activist to guide people to participate actively in the planning process.

We realized now after 40 years of experience, since the introduction of Community Development Projects in the fifties that without active public participation, no plan could be successfully implemented to achieve our goals. Long-term planning should be substituted for short-term and medium-term planning so that people are not frustrated. For political expediency at times planning and development are to be spontaneous; but politicians ought to be careful that before public announcement of any ad hoc decision is made they consult the architect or planner so that viable alternative solutions could be examined.

The architect-planner should be able to prepare an overall structural plan within which the development can take place according to certain guidelines. The requirements of the development plans have to be worked out from the very grassroot levels of the communities. The Gram Panchayats and Zilla Parishads will be the instruments in the formulation and development of the development plan which has to be based on the actual demands and requirements of the communities. The District Administrator, who is the Chairman of the District Planning and Development Board, can have the help of an architect or a planner who can effectively work as a Coordinating Secretary, as by education and training he is better fitted to work in such a multi-development Planning Authority. It must be remembered that one of the causes of failure of our Community Development Schemes launched in the fifties is that there was hardly any effective technical guidance available to the Block Development Officers, who were completely unfamiliar with the tectonically aspects of plan formulation and development.

We are talking about Conservation and Sustainable Development. At the same time we are globalizing our economy to remove poverty, unemployment, social disintegration and environmental degradation, etc., but we still have not seen the light at the other end of the tunnel and we do not know how soon we shall see it. In the meantime, we the poor and the middle class are paying through our noses to welcome indiscriminate foreign capitals to come and save us. Our slogan is only to produce and sell without caring at what cost. They think, it might aggravate rather than alleviate the present global crisis. They even suspect that this neo-liberal system as universal model for development of our economy might not bring the desired goal.

We have to be careful that we do not fall easy prey to so-called consumerism and deplete our scarce resources faster and regret later. We architects and town planners who are responsible for using land must be consciously judicious in exploiting scarce resources for development in the interest of the survival of the nation as we have only about one acre of usable land per capita and our population is still growing. I am grateful to the Institute's President Mr Thimmaiah and the Vice President, Mr. Chairman of the Northern Chapter and members of various committees for arranging this function to felicitate me and giving me the opportunity to my thoughts on some of the problems did we architects share in common.[9]

[9] Journal of The Indian Institute of Architects, May-June 1995, Volume 60, ISSUE 04, Editor Anil Nagrath

"Good Architecture is
the Fusion of Emotion
and Intellect"

— *Jugal Kishore Chowdhury*

Q. What was your response on receiving the highest award of "Indian Institute of Architects" Baburao Mhatre Gold Medal?

A. I was surprised. The news came rather suddenly. I am indeed happy that IIA has conferred this honour on me. I always prefer to work silently.

Q. What are the basic issues of concern to the Profession?

A. Our profession has not come up to the level of our expectations even after forty seven years of independence. Unlike the architects of advanced countries, architects in India have not been able to take full responsibility from design to the completion stage. In advanced countries, license to practice as an Architect is given only to one who has attained sufficient experience and maturity after completing his academic studies. In the USA, it takes 6–12 years. In our country we give license to practice soon after graduation. This is wrong. The Council of Architecture must change this policy. We are a small country with a very large population which is still growing. We must be conscious of judicious use of land and consider it a National Commodity if we want to survive. We must plan use of every inch of land carefully. Our politicians who are responsible for framing land use policy must be made fully aware of this problem.

Q. Basically you are an architect-planner and you have made significant contribution in Architecture and Town Planning, but what is your contribution in Regional Planning?

A. It is true my contribution in Regional Planning cannot be seen in any tangible form. But my background of studies in Tennessee and TVA made me conscious of the importance of coordinated socioeconomic and physical development. The isolated and chaotic developments that we see around us make me feel very unhappy. As President of the Institute of Town Planners India, I strived to influence planners and thinkers to accept regional planning and land use planning as the basis of all developments. Many Five Year Plans have been formulated, but emphasis on regional planning has not been adequate and clear. An overpopulated country like ours where land–population ratio is critical, we cannot tolerate any more delay in our actions to protect our land from misuse, if we want to be self-sufficient in food and live in a healthy environment. Problems are getting multiplied everyday as human beings are the biggest pollutants. We must accept regional planning on the basis of all our developments – social, economic and physical – emphasizing the need for conservation of land and resources and preventing ecological and environmental disaster. We should avoid falling easy prey to consumerism and thus deplete our resources rapidly.

Q. According to you, what is "good architecture and who is a good architect"?

A. To me good architecture is that which does not create conflict between head and heart or between reason and emotion or thinking and feeling. It should be the synthesis or fusion of both emotion and intellect.

A good architect is the one who has the knowledge of planning, construction, structure and services and who can use them imaginatively to produce a work of art and harmony resolving the conflict between head and heart.

Q. Which project of yours is most dear to you?

A. I consider that the Indian Institute of Technology New Delhi is perhaps the work of maturity and some originality, where many architectural problems have been resolved to my satisfaction. My

Jugal Kishore Chowdhury in conversation with Atul Gupta and Abhijit Ray (Journal of The Indian Institute of Architects, May-June 1995, Volume 60, ISSUE 04, Editor Anil Nagrath, Associate editor Harshad Bhatia, Interviewed by Atul Gupta and Abhijit Ray, page 13)

aim was to inspire the engineers studying in the Institute to live, work and play in a creative and congenial atmosphere. I hope I have succeeded to some extent.

Q. You have worked closely with Corbusier but your works didn't reflect his architecture. What is your philosophy of design?
A. Yes, Corbusier was great, but my architecture is my own. Consciously, I never copy Corbusier, though I like the architectural quality of his work. I believe in 'Form Follows Function'. To me every building is a challenge to produce a work of art and originality. But constraints of time and fees and lack of patronage of most clients prevent an architect to give more time in his creative work.

Q. What is the most difficult thing to do in Architecture?
A. To design a client's house. A client has his own ideas and idiosyncrasies. It is often difficult to reconcile them with architect's own ideas. It takes a long time to make his client understand the language of art and architecture. But once you succeed in getting him around and make him understand, you have achieved not only your objective of designing him a beautiful house to live comfortably but also you win him as your life-time friend.

Q. What are your feelings about architectural education in India?
A. Architectural education in India must change radically with the society's need. Ecology and environment should be taught as a subject. Students should be familiar with the History of Arts and Culture of East and West. Analytical study of the past Masters' work including Indian is a must. We should familiarize ourselves with Indian philosophy and culture and also understand the different yardsticks of looking at art and architecture of East and West. Architectural thesis should be research oriented rather than design oriented.

Q. What is your message to the younger generation?
A. I would like to tell our young friends that an architect's work is a reflection of his mind and feelings. An architect must be true to himself. Architecture is a profession and a service to the country and people demanding total involvement, not a business.

Q. These days there is much talk about Vastushastra, what are your feelings about it?
A. We have neglected to study critically and try to understand the basic principles involved in these treatises known as 'Vastushastra'. It is time we reflect on our indigenous art and architecture by introducing courses of studies in our schools.

Q. What according to you is the role of professional bodies like Indian Institute of Architects and Council of Architects in the development of the profession of architecture?
A. Professionally bodies play a key role in development of the profession. IIA is the only professional body capable of looking after development of the profession on the right lines. It should therefore take immediate steps to serve the profession better and upgrade this noble profession. Membership of IIA should be increased. All architects must be members of the professional body. COA has not been able to advance the course architect's adequately. The main purpose of COA ought to regulate registrations of architects only after they pass the qualifying tests to be conducted by IIA. The present constitution of COA is ill-conceived due to our short-sightedness. We should now change it following example of advanced countries. If this is achieved, quality of architecture will improve rapidly.

12
The Legacy

"*For architecture truly reflects one's mind and spirit. It reveals one's inner self and the culture of the society he belongs to. At the same tune, it makes me think, how deep rooted is my architecture to Indian tradition, art and culture. I believe if architecture is to be a living art, then it must continuously change with the times. Each country has its own deep-rooted culture. Therefore, I believe each country's culture should reflect on its architecture to give its identity. Otherwise, the world will be monotonous to live in. Therefore, I think cultural identity in architecture is perhaps necessary.*"

— J K Chowdhury

The architect, who has said this, indeed believed in his words and created wonders accordingly. The respect with which the Jahanpanah wall in IIT Delhi Campus was used and interpreted in the overall campus plan vindicates his stand.

When we started this journey, Jugal Kishore Chowdhury was but a faded image, one who had helmed many prestigious projects which have been long forgotten. In the course of this research, what has emerged is the astounding dedication and insight of the man in creating a modern Indian identity in architecture in the post-Independence era. His quest to design institutions to international standards as well as his vision of sustainable growth of cities in the 1960s is truly overwhelming.

His own speeches and interviews illuminate how far ahead he was of his times. His concepts were simple, functional, aesthetically pleasing and climatically suitable. His approach to architecture and planning is as relevant today as it was then.

What more does one need? The truly modern Indian identity through architecture sought by Mr. Chowdhury is getting lost in the steel and glass structures of today. We hope that this small effort will serve as a memory bank with the power to enable us to rethink our approach towards architecture and sustainable urban planning.

In January 2015, with the great initiation of Jugal Kishore Chowdhury charitable and educational trust and with the help of Dalmia Bharat cement and SPA Delhi, the first memorial lecture of Jugal Kishore Chowdhury was held in Guwahati, which was followed by an exhibition which showcases the work of Jugal Kishore Chowdhury and a publication of a booklet. Eminent speakers like Author Patrick French, S. K. Das were the key speakers of that event.

On 23rd March 2017, the same exhibition was put up at Ansal University, with a panel discussion coordinated by The Dean SSAA, Dr. Vibhuti Sachedva. The panelist were, Prof. E.F.N. Ribeiro, Prof. A. M. Ganju, Prof. Nalini Thakur, Prof. Manoj Mathur, Vijay Garg and each spoke about JKC's work and his relevance today.

The concept of this book was initiated from the overwhelming response of the visitors who saw the exhibition and a need was felt to catalogue the available works and to formulate a book, so that it is accessible to all.

Jugal Kishore Chowdhury's passion was not limited to architecture alone. He had varied interests ranging from arts, culture and music to gardening or cooking. He was fond of all kinds of aesthetic beauty and he appreciated good living and perfection. Being a self-made person, he valued education most of all and offered recognition and encouragement whenever someone in the family excelled in academics. He was also a keen reader and had an in-depth knowledge of the Nath religion and culture. He donated his entire collection of books to the "Nath Cultural and Research Centre," which he established in Guwahati in 1995, three years prior to his death. Over fifty years in the field, Padma Shri Chowdhury served in various capacities and greatly influenced town planning and design of major public projects in the country. He died on 16th December 1998. He was 80. His creation in brick and mortar will speak of his greatness for all time to come.